To Noreen
to my special special
friend.. have a
~ Hazel - Dick - A "Year

Love
Sid Frier

HOW TO MAKE MONEY TOMORROW MORNING

HOW TO MAKE MONEY TOMORROW MORNING

Sid Friedman's SALES SUCCESS SYSTEM

SIDNEY A. FRIEDMAN, CLU, CH FC, RHU

Dearborn
Financial Publishing, Inc.

While a great deal of care has been taken to provide accurate and current information, the ideas, suggestions, general principles and conclusions presented in this book are subject to local, state and federal laws and regulations, court cases and any revisions of same. The reader is thus urged to consult legal counsel regarding any points of law—this publication should not be used as a substitute for competent legal advice.

Publisher: Kathleen A. Welton
Associate Editor: Karen A. Christensen
Cover Design: Lucy Jenkins

© 1992 by Sidney A. Friedman

Published by Dearborn Financial Publishing, Inc.

Printed in the United States of America

92 93 94 10 9 8 7 6 5 4 3 2 1

Library of Congress Cataloging-in-Publication Data

Friedman, Sidney A., 1935–
    How to make money tomorrow morning : Sid Friedman's sales success
system / Sidney A. Friedman.
        p. cm.
    Includes Index.
    ISBN 0-7931-0292-8
    1. Insurance, Life—Agents. 2. Selling. 3. Success in business.
    I. Title.
HG8876.F75 1991
368'.0068'8—dc20   91-26908
                                                            CIP

Dedication

To my honey, Sue, whom I affectionately call Becky, and to the best two kids in the whole world, Lori and Wendi, who allow me the time to do what I love to do.

Acknowledgments

To all the salespeople
worldwide who
taught me something special

From Boro Park in Brooklyn, New York, where life began for me, to so many parts of the earth, I have met some of the best salespeople of all kinds, especially life insurance salespeople.

From each, I was taught something. Here and there I gathered little bits of the many wonderful sales ideas, concepts, and sales tracks that I use. I cannot wait until tomorrow to learn some more.

I dedicate this book to all these people of my past:

To Benny and Celie, my mom and dad. How special he was and she is. They taught me values, integrity, and loyalty.

To Dave Jacobs, my mom's brother, who started my insurance career and showed me relationship building and customer services par excellence.

To all the people at the Keystone Agency in Philadelphia who helped launch my career with their undying integrity and loyalty. They say we represented the Phoenix Mutual Life Insurance Company, but we really represented each other. What a sales team, the best in the business!

To the AALU, CLU, GAMA, MDRT, The Forum, The Top of The Table, and the thousands of people I have had the privilege of addressing through speeches and seminars around the world.

To Frank Freudberg, who helped me put my ideas in order and on paper.

And finally, to my special friend, Mike Ferguson of MDRT, who passed away in June.

To all these people (and those I'll learn from in the future) my thanks and my undying respect.

Table of Contents

Preface

The information contained in this book can be put to work right away—as early as tomorrow morning. *How To Make Money Tomorrow Morning* contains a powerful message that is as simple as it is direct: Carefully—very carefully—determine what you want out of life and life insurance sales; learn to dream about your goals in great detail; create a logical plan to make it happen; and then never, ever, let up.

I will use every dramatic method I can to drive my message home to you: I'll show the same idea from as many different views as possible; I'll tell you stories and quote great people; and I'll reveal over 100 specific techniques—my "trade secrets"—to help you make sales right away.

Ten words—each having only two letters—are at the heart of this book. Learn these words, believe in them, and you are bound to succeed.

> ## *If it is to be, it is up to me.*

The vehicle that I used to turn my dreams into reality is the art of selling life insurance. The great "secrets" of my success are described in detail in this book. They are here to help you make money. Immediately.

These ideas, by the way, have been around for a long time. I don't own them. No one owns them. Remember the saying, "If you take an idea from one person, it is called stealing. If you take many ideas from many people, it is called research." I am a great researcher!

As you read on, you will learn that this book contains no requirements for success that you cannot achieve simply by trying and doing. None.

My life and my successes are proof that by using sheer determination and by never letting up, you can make your dreams come true. Never let up, and you will succeed. Guaranteed.

> ## *WARNING: This book is unique!*

There are hundreds—probably thousands—of books out there about selling. Many of these books are written by bona fide experts and are quite valuable for the knowledge they impart.

Almost all of them follow a common format: The author discusses prospecting first, selling next, and then closes the book. Some of the more contemporary books throw in material about customer service.

My book is different.

This book, although it covers all these subjects and more, does not deliver information in cut-and-dried categories. The ideas I present here are not linked subject-by-subject, but in the way that they occur in the real world of selling. The real world of selling is the world of having people on the other end of the telephone hang up on you; of working twelve-hour days, six or seven days a week; and of dreaming a dream and then watching it come true beyond your wildest wishes.

Who Can Benefit from This Book?

This book is designed for two kinds of people: those who are already in the business insurance market and who want some simple sales ideas to increase their personal production; and those who are not yet in the business insurance market but who want to be.

This book provides ideas about selling to business executives in their office environment versus selling to married couples in their living room.

If you are used to selling to individuals in their homes, then you probably have plenty of time to work more hours during the day because you only work at night. On the other hand, if you are used to selling to business executives during the daytime, then you definitely should intensify your efforts to see more and more business people—when possible—in the evenings. This book can help you get to see more of these people because you'll be armed with first-class sales ideas.

I hope that this book infuses you with a true spirit of success—however that spirit manifests itself in you. If I have helped you move even one inch closer to finding your own spirit of success, then I have done my job.

—SIDNEY A. FRIEDMAN

Don't Be Afraid To Fail

You've failed
many times,
although you may not
remember.
You fell down
the first time
you tried to walk.
You almost drowned
the first time
you tried to
swim, didn't you?
Did you hit the
ball the first time
you swung a bat?
Heavy hitters,
the ones who hit the
most home runs,
also strike
out a lot.
R.H. Macy
failed seven
times before his
store in New York
caught on.
English novelist
John Creasey got
753 rejection slips
before he published
564 books.
Babe Ruth struck out
1,330 times,
but he also hit
714 home runs.
Don't worry about
failure.
Worry about the
chances you miss
when you don't
even try.

Introduction

By reading and thinking about *How To Make Money Tomorrow Morning,* you will get a clearer understanding of what it takes to be a success in the life insurance business. To succeed in this business, it certainly takes sales ideas—good, creative, original sales ideas—but it also takes a great deal of perseverance and discipline.

The principles in this book are innovative, but they are also simple. Read the book, dream your dream (and, as I'll explain later, learn to dream it in *color*), develop a plan of action, and discipline yourself to make it happen—and it will.

I strongly suggest that you *take notes* as you read this book. Sometimes ideas that aren't immediately written down are forgotten. In addition, this book may spark your own creative ideas about selling. Having a pen and notebook handy ensures that you'll retain your own ideas and put them to good use. The habit of note taking is a good one to develop. Wherever you are, whatever you do, you can learn something, even if what you learn is what *not* to do! *Write it down right away.*

> ***These ideas are universal. They apply to life as well as life insurance.***

The ideas in my book apply to selling anything. The discipline required to achieve great success in life insurance applies to sales processes of any kind, in any field, in any endeavor.

In this book I discuss selling life insurance because that is what I do, but sales are sales. Therefore, these ideas apply to many sales situations.

A Little Bit about How I Started

My own experience illustrates how great expectations lead to success.

I began my career in the insurance business while I was still in high school and working at my uncle's agency in Brooklyn. From the start, I loved talking to people and providing them with the things they needed. It was a challenge, a battle of wits. It wasn't so much that I wanted to fast-talk them into something (although back then that was how most insurance policies were sold), but that I was genuinely interested in learning something about their lives. I was naturally curious about what they wanted, what they expected, and what they hoped for from life. I wanted to know what their dreams were. Once I had that down, I tried to provide them the insurance product that they really needed.

That small, part-time job evolved into a full-time career once I graduated from New York University. From there, I went on to Brooklyn Law School.

Working for my uncle was a great learning experience that helped me launch a lucrative career. By the time I was about 30 years old in 1965, I was making $40,000 a year—not bad for the times and certainly enough to inspire many people to stay put.

But I wanted more.

The world seemed too exciting to spend my life working for someone else. At the same time, my uncle had brought his immediate family into the business. I was third in line from the top—a position that did not appeal to me.

So for the first—and only—time in my life, I scanned the help wanted ads. A three-line ad in *The New York Times* caught my attention.

The ad was placed by two sales managers from Phoenix Mutual Life Insurance Company. One had an office in Queens, New York—only minutes from my home. The other had an office in Norwalk, Connecticut. The ad said they were eager for quality recruits. The system that they set up called for Monday's leads from the ads to go to the Queens office. On Tuesdays, the leads went to Norwalk, and so on throughout the week. As bad luck would have it, my name went to Norwalk—an hour's drive from the city. But I made the trip, and I liked what I heard: a sales and management job.

The job offered a lot of opportunity, but the pay was only 60 percent of what I was making then. That concerned me because I had just gotten married, and my wife Sue was six months pregnant. But instead of walking out, I was struck by the idea that I could really make the job work.

"I'll take the job," I told them, "but only if there is a real chance for me to get my own agency."

You see, I visualized myself in offices like those that the sales managers had.

The Phoenix Mutual people smugly agreed, but said that I would have to meet their sales objectives to prove that I deserved my own office.

They laid out the deal and gave me two years to reach the goals of recruiting, training, and personal sales. The goals sounded reasonable to me, but I didn't really have the experience to know whether they were attainable.

Years later, I learned that the sales manager had purposely set the goals so high that he just assumed they could never be reached. But my bosses didn't know the power of my desire to succeed or what a person can achieve when he or she believes that something really can happen!

I threw myself into the work with all the power and conviction I could muster. This was my first real chance to prove myself. I wasn't going to let it slip away. I was going to work really hard to achieve my mission and earn an agency of my own.

Every morning, I would get up at 5:15 and leave the house by 5:45. I didn't like it at first, but I grew to love it. By seven o'clock I was already at my desk preparing things for my agents, who usually got to work at about 7:30.

The entire office would then spend the next hour doing paper work and preparing for the day. We held sales meetings and pep rallies—whatever it took to get us ready to win.

An hour later, at 8:30, I was on the road with my agents, dual selling. I would stay in the field until eight or nine o'clock. I never took a short day or a day off. I didn't define the work day by hours. Instead, I determined the amount of work that needed to be accomplished. If that took 20 hours, that is how long I worked.

I would usually get home at about midnight. Sue would be waiting for me with dinner. Incidentally, Sue worked from nine to five, got home and slept for a few hours, woke up at 10 P.M. and made me dinner. Without her, I couldn't have done it. She didn't like my long hours, but she loved me and believed that my hard work would pay off.

No wonder I never let her get away.

It was a brutal schedule that would have destroyed anyone without a burning desire to succeed. But I relished it and did everything possible to stay positive. For instance, on the way to work I played motivational tapes on a battery-powered tape recorder. Through the voices of greats like Ben Feldman, Maxwell Maltz,

Larry Wilson, Dennis Waitley, and countless other successful sales-persons and motivational speakers, I learned about adversity, chal-lenge, and success. Listening to them was like mainlining pure motivation. My heart would pound with their messages. By the time I reached work, I was ready to take on the world, confident that each day would bring new achievements.

The effort paid off.

With each passing day and week, I made headway. What at first seemed impossible became more and more plausible. It was all based on how hard I worked and how positive I remained.

We started to sell a lot more policies. My agents became market-ing machines, bringing back policy after policy. The more success-ful they became, the more successful I became. I devoted six days a week to nurturing them, urging them, training them, and reassur-ing them of their self-worth. On the seventh day of each week, I would go out and sell for myself and meet with personal clients who I had been too busy to see during the week.

To the astonishment of my supervisors, I raced closer and closer to what at one time was their "impossible-to-attain" sales goals. Within six months, I had reached the objectives we set down at the start of my employment. To them, I had achieved the impossible—*18 months ahead of schedule.*

The top dogs were dumbfounded. They couldn't believe what I had done or how fast I had done it. It was time for them to pay up. I had kept my end of the bargain. I had earned an agency of my own, and in typical youthful brazenness, I demanded it immedi-ately.

At the time, there were 60 Phoenix Mutual offices located across the country. I wanted a region with potential. Boy, did I get one: I got the Philadelphia office, the company's worst-performing agency, number 60 on the list of performers.

Despite this, Philadelphia became my home for the next 25 years. Before I arrived the office had been woefully neglected and poorly managed for years. It had first-year commissions of less than $30,000, a number I would increase tenfold during the first three years of management.

When I arrived, however, the office was an abomination. It wasn't so much that it was unproductive—hell, there was no pro-ductivity. Most of the 24 agents were right out of the movie *Tin Men*. They were crass and unprofessional. Most held other jobs, like selling shoes or cars. They used the office as a stopover point for their many other occupations and preoccupations.

Making it even worse was the fact that Philadelphia was as foreign to me as Madagascar. I had rarely been out of the New York area. I knew Brooklyn, Queens, Long Island, and Connecticut, but not much more. I was facing a new marriage, a new child, a new job, and a new city.

Many young, hotshot sales professionals would have recoiled from the offer. They probably would have seen it as more of a nightmare than an opportunity. But, remember, I was totally determined. Not once did I even consider the downside. This was the biggest opportunity of my career. The fact that the office was underperforming made the upside that much more attractive.

I went to Philadelphia in December 1966 on one condition: I insisted that I be allowed to keep the office's net profit at the end of the year.

The vice presidents at Phoenix Mutual gladly obliged. They probably thought that there would be no net profits and that I was asking for nothing.

They were wrong. Office performance was a turnaround reminiscent of the Chrysler Motors story.

I spent the first month sequestered in my office, reviewing every morsel of information about the agency.

Who were the agents?

Where did they come from?

How much did they earn?

What was the overhead?

How many support staffers were there?

What did they do and how did they spend their time?

Who hired and fired these people?

What was at the heart of the office's problems?

How could I fix it?

At the end of the month I fired 21 of the 24 agents.

They pouted. They threatened me. They called the home office and reported me. They ran to other agencies in Philadelphia with wild stories of the crazy kid from New York who thought he knew everything.

But I didn't care. They had been hired to sell, and they did not perform. I didn't let any of it affect me. Sure, it would have been easier not to rock the boat so violently. I could have muddled through for a year, slowly rebuilding the company. But I was inspired by a deep desire to succeed—and to do so quickly.

The day after the purge I walked through the empty offices and started planning the reconstruction. I began hiring that afternoon. As amazing as it sounds, four of the people I hired during those first few months are still with me today—a fact that I consider one of my greatest accomplishments. It speaks volumes about the way to treat and respect people.

The Philadelphia office went on to become the most successful Phoenix Mutual office, consistently winning awards and setting sales records through the years. The Philadelphia office has become a benchmark for Phoenix Mutual and the life insurance industry in general.

None of this would have been possible without the crazy, relentless determination that makes up a good chunk of what Sid Friedman is all about. I refused to live my life and manage my business as others wanted me to. I approached each day as a crazy, new adventure—an outlook that ultimately led me to the pinnacles of the insurance industry as well as a multimillion-dollar annual income.

Can you do it, too?

Can you apply the principles of success to increase your productivity, to become a better salesperson, and to attain and surpass your goals for personal and financial achievement?

If you said "no," then you have a lot of work to do!

If you said "yes," then you are well on your way to achieving your goals. You may not know exactly what to do yet. But hang on. Stick with me. I want to share my ideas with you.

Should I be worried about giving away my trade secrets?

Hell, no!

The volume of business out there is ridiculously high. The more, the merrier. All we can do is help each other, give life insurance a better name, make more money, and help more people.

I want to end this autobiographical section with this idea: Don't ever settle for the typical, for the obvious, for the easily attainable. Reach out past boundaries and dare to be great.

Sound crazy?

Of course it is, but that's the point of this exercise. You can't be a regular man or woman and achieve super success in the sales arena. You must be different, atypical, abnormal. There is positively no way you can achieve greatness by following the same, tired course walked by thousands before you. You must forge your own way into the forest and clear your own trails.

If greatness is your goal, if you long for a degree of success that will astound even you, then this is the way it must be. You must promise a lot, and deliver even more! In short, and without even the slightest fear of being considered egocentric, I tell you, to succeed, you must be like me.

Part One

Great Expectations

1 Promise a Lot... and Deliver More

If one advances confidently in the direction of his dreams, and endeavors to live the life which he has imagined, he will meet with a success unexpected in common hours.

—HENRY DAVID THOREAU

The idea of promising a lot and delivering much more is easily the most important issue of this book.

Make promises very carefully.

Make sure you can deliver.

If you promise a client something, do it.

Many people promise a lot and deliver very little or nothing at all. Others promise a lot and deliver something mediocre. My philosophy is to promise a lot and deliver even more than you promised.

If you promise to give clients a certain level of service annually, do it quarterly.

If you promise to call them by Thursday, call them by Wednesday.

If you promise to be there at nine o'clock in the morning, be there at 8:45.

You offer a certain level of service to clients. It is your promise. Make sure you deliver on that promise, no matter what. If for some reason something goes wrong—and things do go wrong at times—be sure to make up for it to your client. Call the client in advance to explain what went wrong. Apologize so that the client knows it's an accident. Let your client know that what happened was the exception, not the rule.

Delivering on Your Promises

After you've gotten the order, you must do what you promised. Delivering on your promises is an incredibly important part of the sales process.

You promise a lot. Now, deliver more.

3

What you tell the client you are going to do, you must do. You must do it in spades. But you also must do more than you promised, because that's what builds an agency's reputation and its sales.

The prospect must believe that you care so much that you are willing—even happy—to provide more than you promised.

If you told your client that a policy's cash value in 20 years would be $100,000, when it really would be $110,000, that's wonderful.

If you said that the policy would vanish in eight years and it vanishes in seven, that's wonderful.

If you said that you would deliver something in two weeks, and you deliver in a week and a half, that's even better.

Promise a lot, and deliver more.

••

Trade Secret #1

How Can I Promise a Lot and Deliver More Myself?

What are some ways you can go that extra mile and do that little bit extra to really serve your prospects? The following questions will help you think about what you can do.

1. What kind of promises can I honestly make to provide my prospect with more value? (check those that apply, and then add your own)

    a. Faster delivery time _____
    b. More follow-up _____
    c. Better service on repairs _____
    d. A longer warranty period _____
    e. Special presentations to personal contacts _____
    f. Assistance with use of product or service _____
    g. A newsletter or updates on service _____
    h. A money-back guarantee _____
    i. Using testimonials or references from satisfied customers to provide better service to others _____
    j. Special programs/events for customers _____

k. Other (write in your own) _____

_____

_____

_____

_____

_____

2. How can I show my prospect that my product or service offers more than is available elsewhere? (check those that apply, and then add your own)

a. Better product features than the competition offers (note which ones)

_____

_____

b. Better servicing than the competition offers (note which ones)

_____

_____

••

2 The Story of an Unexpected Salesperson

If it ain't broke, break it. [Find the flaw in your prospect's current insurance program.] *Fix it, and MAKE IT BETTER!*
— SIDNEY FRIEDMAN

I love to tell the story about Bill, whom I met at a Cadillac dealership.

My daughter, Lori, had a car accident as she was driving her Nissan 280Z home from Atlantic City. Traffic was heavy, and the car in front of her stopped very short. Lori stopped in time, but the car behind hers didn't. It smashed into her car and pushed it into the car in front of hers. She was almost thrown out of the car through the T roof. Her car was wrecked, but she was lucky. She didn't get thrown out, and the car could still be driven.

The car was brought to my house in Cherry Hill and I called the Cadillac/Nissan dealership where we got it. "We've had a major accident," I said to the man on the other end of the line.

"Can the car be driven?"

"Yep."

"Then bring it in."

"OK, but I can't get there till Friday night at about ten o'clock." He told me that they closed at about six.

"What can we do?" I asked.

The dealer said that the night watchman, Bill, would be there. "He just cleans the place up, but he'll accept the car."

I asked for a loaner to take home. The dealer assured me that they would find me a car—not a new car, but one that would get me home.

My wife, Sue, and I drove Lori's car to the dealership on Friday night. The car was clanking all the way. After an hour-long ride we arrived and found that all the lights were out in the dealership except for one in the parking lot. Inside we saw a man about 55 years old in overalls and suspenders with rags hanging out of his pockets. He was doing the floors with a waxing machine.

"Are you, Bill?" I asked.

"Yes, sir, I am."

"Bill, my name is—"

"I know what your name is," he interrupted. "Your name is Mr. Friedman. You came to bring your daughter's car."

"That's right. It's 11 o'clock at night, Bill. Do you have another car for me to take home so I can leave this one?"

"Certainly do. You have to come in and sign some papers. Can you come inside?"

I went inside and left Sue in the car.

Bill turned on all the lights in the showroom of the huge dealership. The cars looked like they went on for two or three blocks.

"Mr. Friedman, please come with me for a minute."

He was up to something, but I didn't care to know what it was at that hour.

"I'm really tired, Bill. I want to get the car and I want to go home. It's Friday night, I'm tired, I've been working all day."

"Mr. Friedman, just come with me. I want to show you something."

I asked him to just give me the papers.

"I will, in a minute," he said.

He took me to the other end of the showroom—which seemed a mile-long hike. He showed me a brand new Corinthian blue Cadillac convertible, its roof down revealing its white leather interior.

"What do you think of this car?" he asked.

"Bill, I'm tired. I really do want to go home. Would you let me have my car, the car you've got to give me, so that I can go home?"

I couldn't figure him out. What did he want me to do, buy him a Cadillac because he let me in after hours?

"Just a minute," he said. "Indulge me."

He opened the door of the car.

"Mr. Friedman, would you sit down in this car?"

The showroom lights were all pouring down on the beautiful, metallic blue car with its sweet-smelling new leather interior.

I was getting steamed up.

"Bill, I don't want to see the car. I've got more cars than I have drivers right now."

"Just sit down in the car," he insisted.

I thought he was a real pain, and I intended to tell the dealer about him first thing Monday morning. On the other hand, I knew that I had to patronize him just to get out of there.

I sat down in the car. He closed the door behind me and told me to look up. Up in the ceiling, were mirrors.

"How does it feel to sit behind the wheel of a brand new Cadillac convertible?"

At last his purpose was clear. I started to laugh.

By that time Sue had joined us. He opened the other door for Sue to get in. There we were, sitting in a showroom in a parked Cadillac and being cajoled by the dealership's night watchman at 11 o'clock at night.

Sue and I talked about the car.

"Sue, it is a gorgeous car."

She agreed but pointed out that we didn't need another car. We had all the cars we could use.

Finally, Bill released his hostages. I guess he figured he'd planted the seed. We were driving home in the used car that was left for us. All we talked about on the way home was the spectacular Corinthian blue Caddie that we sure didn't need.

I've got a Rolls Royce. Sue's got a Mercedes Benz. We share a chauffeur-driven limousine. We didn't need another car.

You can probably guess what happened: The seed sprouted.

By the next Tuesday night, the car was parked in my driveway in Cherry Hill.

I called the owner on Monday and told him that I would buy the car under two conditions: one, that they give the standard commission to Bill; and two, that they give me a good price.

I got a good price, and Bill got the commission.

Mission accomplished.

Three weeks later, Bill called.

What was he going to sell me this time? I wondered.

"Mr. Friedman," he said, "I'm calling because it's been three weeks since you got the car. I know something's got to be wrong with it. New cars have things go wrong. Pieces fall out, something rattles. They don't mean to make them that way, but they do.

"I want to come pick up your car. I want to bring it back here to the dealership. I want to see what I can do to make it right. Then I'll bring it back to you again."

Usually by the time I have to bring my car into a dealership, I'm already in deep trouble. They normally can't fix my problem, and they have millions of excuses. They can't get this part or that part. This guy's on vacation or that guy's out sick.

All of a sudden here was a man who wanted to come to my house, pick up my car, and get it fixed for me.

Bill picked up the car, not because he was a maintenance man or a repair man, but because he was a *salesman.* (Unbeknown to me, the dealership made him a salesman three weeks after he sold me my car—*because* he sold me my car.)

He picked up the car and made a list of the things that were wrong. Later that day, he brought it back with everything fixed.

Three months went by. Bill called again. "I want to pick up your car. I want to bring it back."

He picked up the car at my office and brought it back later in perfect condition—and washed. It was sparkling like it was just off the showroom floor. He washed it personally.

Bill not only got my business, he led the entire northeast corridor of Cadillac Motorcar in sales for 1986. He sold more cars than anyone in that zone ever had. In 1987, he sold 350 cars. He's probably retired now—this was about six years ago.

When somebody asked me about a car and I knew Bill was working, I couldn't wait to pick up the phone and call him. Bill promised a lot and delivered more. He kept on delivering so much that I almost felt obligated to refer prospective car buyers to him. He cared so much that I wanted to help him. Bill was a class act, the personification of what the concept of "promise a lot and deliver more" means to me.

••

Trade Secret #2

Showing Prospects You're Aware

Let your prospects know that you are thinking about them. Sending them newspaper or magazine clippings on topics relevant to their businesses (changes in a tax law, swings in the real estate market, a new development in health care) is a first class way to show your prospects that you know what their problems are and that you are alert for ways to solve them.

Attach your unique business card to the clipping along with a short note on down-sized letterhead (4" × 5" instead of the standard 8.5" × 11"). They will appreciate that you care and are interested.

••

3 The Two Requirements for Success

Luck is where preparation and opportunity meet.

—CHINESE PROVERB

I want to inspire you to have tremendous confidence in yourself and in your ability to be wildly successful. I hope that you will have great expectations about yourself.

There are only two requirements.

First, you must want to succeed. Or let me rephrase that slightly: You must *need* to succeed. Merely wanting something is fine, but if you just *want* something then it is pretty easy to get distracted. When trouble arises you can kid yourself by deciding that you now want something different than your original goal. You have to *need* to succeed.

Second, you must follow a proven plan. Obviously, I know a plan that works, the plan I developed for myself. And I know it can work for you if you follow it. You could probably use other proven plans devised by people who have succeeded. I cannot vouch for those plans. I know my only plan, how it works, why it works, and when it works. It is not the only plan, but it is *a* plan, that will make you a super successful life insurance agent.

I challenge you to follow the theories of sales success that I have laid out in this book. If you take the challenge and work at it you'll succeed. When you do succeed, do me a favor and send a letter telling me about your success. (My mailing address is The Bellevue, 220 S. Broad St., Philadelphia, PA 19102.) Tell me what you do now that you didn't do before you read my ideas. Tell me about the things you used to do that you don't do anymore.

Your letter will go together with the other similar letters I have received from people I've helped. Those letters are very important to me. I cherish them. They inspire *me* when I'm feeling down.

If you choose to accept my challenge, then your task is to emulate my success by invoking your own sense of creativity and uniqueness. I want you to bring your own individuality into the picture. This book can help, but only if you can take the positive steps to achieve success—however you, personally, define success.

10

•••

Trade Secret #3

Winners and Losers

To paraphrase William Shakespeare, "There are no such things as winners or losers—only behavior makes it so."

I agree. Anyone can become the person that they want to be if enough determination and will are brought into the picture. Studying those who are winners, however, shows specific common traits in their approaches to life and life insurance.

Winners	*Versus*	*Losers*
Keep going		Give up
Are decisive		Are uncertain
Act quickly		Hesitate
See the big picture		Bog down in details
Act		Procrastinate
Set high goals		Set easily attainable goals
Are confident		Have low self-esteem
Win some, lose some, continue		Win some, lose some, get hung up on the failures
Are like thermostats—they set the temperature		Are like thermometers—just react

•••

4 *Keep Swinging*

Keep working your plan everyday—even when you don't feel like it—and you will be AMAZED at how soon it begins to pay off.

—SIDNEY FRIEDMAN

I'll tell you a story that Ben Friedman, my father, told me.

It's a true story that I first heard when I was about ten years old. My father told the story until the day he died when I was 50. I'm now 56, and it hasn't lost any relevance.

In Yiddish there's an expression that means if you chop wood, splinters will fly. The meaning of the expression is in the story.

"Sonny," my dad told me, "if there's a log of wood in front of you—a big log in front of you—and you want to cut that log in half, the first thing you must do is pick up the axe every day. You must swing it. Every day. Rain or shine. And that axe has a blade that has two sides—a dull side and a sharp side.

"You have to pick up the axe every day and swing it. I don't care if you use the dull side of the axe, but you keep swinging. One day, if you chop hard enough and long enough, the splinters will begin to fly. But one day you are going to wake up and say, 'You know what, I'm going to swing the axe just like I do every day. But today I'll swing the blade with the sharp side down.' "

That's the real issue: You have to keep chopping wood every single day. Even if you are unsure of your final goal you'll make progress. No matter what you do, you'll get some splinters, and they'll make you some money. But one day you'll get smart: you'll turn the sharp side down and you'll find that you will really make progress. That's what it's all about.

Keep swinging. I believe that my dad was right.

The Difference Between Being Successful and Mediocre

Is there a difference between a Hall of Famer and a regular old baseball player? Of course there is a major difference in their levels of achievement.

But what makes up that difference is unbelievably small, even shockingly insignificant. But it is this minor difference that makes all the difference in becoming successful.

The difference is really very small and here's what I mean: To get into the Hall of Fame you need about a .350 batting average. But what exactly, in terms of effort, is the difference between a .350 batter and a .260 batter? Well, the truth is that the difference is only one more hit every so many times at bat.

You'd think that this is so simple that everybody would rush right out and do absolutely anything to get that one more hit. But human nature is surprising. There's only a handful of Hall of Famers in the world. The same thing is true for the insurance business.

Whether it's the Million Dollar Round Table or the Top of the Table, it takes only one more hit every so many times at bat.

You have to keep swinging the bat.

Every single chance you get, swing that bat.

The difference between Hall of Famers and others is that the Hall of Famers are willing to do the work that the others won't do. Not can't do. *Won't* do!

Successful people do it every time.

It isn't once in a while or when they feel like it. It isn't when a bill is pressing or when a big vacation is coming up.

Instead, it's consistent. It's routine. It's second nature.

And they keep doing it every day.

•••

Trade Secret #4

The Magic of Two Extra Hours

If you set your alarm clock 50 minutes earlier, cut 20 minutes out of your lunch break, and stay on the job 50 minutes later, you'll add two work hours to each day. That's ten hours added per week if you work five days a week. (I usually work seven.)

Ten extra hours each week comes to 520 extra hours each year. Those 520 extra hours equal 13 normal 40-hour work weeks. Now if you are earning $50,000 a year, that comes to about $1,000 per week. If you simply continue to work at your existing level of efficiency, putting those extra minutes to work is the equivalent of getting a check for $13,000 in the mail. (If you begin to work more effectively, the amount you earn can double, triple, or increase even more!)

I'd set my alarm clock 50 minutes earlier for a check like that. Wouldn't you?

••

5 *When You Aim Low...*
...You Get What You Expect

It is better to aim for the sky and hit the side of the barn than it is to aim for the barn and hit the ground.

—ANONYMOUS

If you aim too low, that's where you'll wind up: too low. You'll get what you aimed for. That's why they say be careful what you wish for, because you might get it.

If you're wishing by aiming too low, that's where you're going to come out. You will be no more than you expect.

What do the folks who aim at the Million Dollar Round Table as a goal, which comes to about $42,000 in commissions, have if they have no dreams to go with the cash?

For whatever reason, lots of people lack enough self-confidence to aim high. For them, the solution is so simple it is scary.

Simply shoot higher.

You only get what you expect.

I know an agent, Larry Edmonds, who told me he wanted to earn $50,000 in commissions his first year in the business. He did it. As a matter of fact, he earned $52,500.

The next year he planned on making $60,000. He surpassed that goal too.

I bumped into him five years later at the airport. He was with his wife and two children, and they were leaving on a vacation to the islands. I asked him how he was doing.

"Great!" he said. "Each year I plan to earn $10,000 more than the previous year. And I haven't failed yet. This year I'm planning on making $110,000, and I'm right on track."

I thought for a minute.

"Larry," I said, "what would happen if you began to plan on increasing your annual commissions by $20,000 each year, instead of $10,000? After all, you've never missed your goal yet. You look like you are getting plenty of sleep, so you probably aren't killing yourself. Do you have time to make another couple of calls each day?"

He thought for a minute. An odd expression came over his face.

15

"Sid," he said, "you've just ruined my vacation. I can't wait for it to be over so I can get back to the office to revise my production goals for this year."

I haven't seen Larry since, but it's a good bet he is still making his goals every year—whatever they are.

••

Trade Secret #5

How To Succeed in Business: Effort

First be absolutely, positively sure that you want to succeed. Then find a plan that is logical, reasonable, and workable. And never let up. *Never.* No matter what obstacles, challenges, and impediments life throws your way.

••

6 *Opportunity Knocks All the Time . . . But Usually Very Softly*

Communication is the right person, saying the right thing, to the right person, at the right place, at the right time, in the right way.

—EDWIN WINTERS

You must always keep your eyes and ears open as you talk to people. If you're doing your job properly, you'll notice parts of conversation that you can seize upon. This skill makes for a winning relationship with a client.

For example, a client might say something like, "I have an employee named John Jones. This guy works his rear end off. He's really good. I'd be lost without him." Seize the opportunity to pitch a key employee approach. "If you'd really be lost without him, insure him. Do it for the benefit of the corporation."

Or suppose a client says, "Gee, I've been to the doctor lately, and thank God my health's good." Take the opportunity to sell disability insurance.

Or if the client tells you that profits are up and that the business is making more money than ever before, talk about a qualified or non-qualified plan to save money from the tax collector.

Suppose that the client says something like, "Gee, my estate's growing by leaps and bounds. I'm worth $5 million today." Point out the tax lien that the IRS has on his or her estate for estate taxes.

Seize the opportunity by thinking about what the client is saying and how it is being said.

Listen.

Listen the client into buying, and keep your antennae up for ideas.

••

Trade Secret #6

Turning Canceled Appointments into New Opportunities

If a prospect cancels an appointment—or if you get inadvertently stood up by a prospect—take advantage of the situation by

17

- Being understanding: "I understand that your urgent meeting was unpredictable."
- Asking for another meeting right away: "Can we get together tomorrow morning?"
- Offering to meet your prospect at his or her convenience: "I know you have a difficult schedule, but I am so sure that this policy is right for you that I am willing to meet you wherever and whenever you can see me."

7 *Success Takes More than a Genie*

I'm a great believer in luck, and I find that the harder I work, the more of it I have!

—CHARLES WEST

Everything in my life seems to break just right. But I'm not naturally lucky.

I make my own luck.

Maybe there's a little genie on my shoulder. How he got there, I don't know. Actually, I like to think that somehow I put him on my shoulder. I like to believe that. I don't know where I found this genie, but he needs care. I take care of him. How?

I do it by understanding his mission.

"I can make good things happen," he says, "but I can't do it alone. Help me to help you by doing the right things. I can't do it alone."

I'm not crazy.

The genie is just a metaphor for good luck. I must work hard to cooperate with him and turn luck into opportunity and success.

••

Trade Secret #7

Who's in Charge Around Here, Anyway?

Work to control interviews with prospects.

If you are in a prospect's home and a television is audible, ask your prospect to turn it off.

If you are in an office and there are a lot of interruptions, ask if your prospect can have phone calls held and the office door closed.

Ask the prospect to do something for you. A request for a glass of water or coffee puts you on the prospect's level and takes you out of the role of just being a salesperson.

••

8 Recognizing and Using Turning Points

When asked how to write a smash hit, a famous Broadway playwright responded, "The same exact way you write a flop."

Sometimes events in your life can give you a clearer vision of what your goals are. Watch for them. The turning points for me were my marriage and the birth of my first daughter, Lori.

I was unwilling to accept mediocrity after those events.

It took the better part of the previous 30 years to decide that I didn't like what I had. Eventually I got a handle on what I wanted. The big changes didn't come overnight, but the little ones—enough to encourage me—came immediately. I felt better about myself right away because I was working harder. That was one change. But it didn't all happen in one fell swoop. Changes came one step at a time. I did one thing that worked, and it led me to try something else. When those things worked, I said, "Hey, this ain't bad," and I tried other things.

I developed the habit of winning and I broke the habit of losing.

Once you start winning, the sweet smell of success keeps you going.

••

Trade Secret #8

Key Qualities of a Professional

Successful professionals share common characteristics. A pro
1. Is good and knows it
2. Always critiques his or her own performance to stop doing what's wrong and to start doing more of what's right
3. Keeps working on getting better

And, importantly, a pro is a conscious competent. That is, professionals know exactly how they are achieving their goals. They are not on automatic pilot. They are consciously competent.

••

20

9 *Prime the Pump*

Good things come to those who wait, but they get what's left over from those who hustle!

—*Anonymous*

In my agency I have a salesman who is 42 years old, and frankly, he never set the world afire selling insurance. I don't mean to say that he's terrible. He's made $50,000 to $70,000 a year. But he is in trouble because he's been spending more than that. He's not meeting his needs.

Through a cold call, an absolute ice-cold call, he found a prospect who owns a $10 million policy. That is great news to any insurance professional. My agent almost went through the roof. He went out to see the prospect. The prospect was a very tough sell. He threw the agent out.

But my agent kept trying and found out the prospect was paying a fortune in premiums. This is an absolute dream to a life insurance salesperson. Why? Because the premiums can always be improved, either by increasing the policy's value or by reducing its premium.

The prospect eventually said he didn't think he bought the right policy and that he wanted to replace it. The agent presented proposals over and over again. The client was still belligerent.

No was the only word he seemed to know.

Finally, they made a deal.

In this one sale the salesman earned $160,000 in commissions, more than he had seen in the last three years of his career.

You might say, "How many times could something like that happen to me?"

My answer?

Once is a damn good place to start!

It happened only because the agent made the phone calls. The harder you work, the luckier you get.

You'd think that after that kind of a sale the agent would understand why I insist that all of my agents make 100 prospecting phone calls each week. But some people are chronically unmotivated.

My agent's just not doing it. He's resting on his laurels and coasting along! He's missing that special ingredient: discipline. He lacks the ability to stick to it. He's just not working. He's not looking for another big hit.

You only get another big hit by making other calls. The agent didn't expect to get a big hit when he made that call. If there's another one in the pile he won't find because he doesn't make the calls.

It's quite a bit like playing the slot machines. When you put in your quarter and pull the handle on a slot machine, you want to get a lot more quarters. It is a question of time and effort. If you pull on the handle long enough, you may get 100 quarters. Invest even more, put in even more effort, and you could get 1,000 quarters.

In a casino, putting the quarter in the slot machine and pulling the arm is your effort. In sales, making those calls is the effort. It isn't easy. Sometimes it can be boring and frustrating. Sometimes it can just drive you crazy. And sometimes one call can get you $160,000.

Prime the pump to get the water. Keep pumping. Don't stop before the water comes out.

•••

Trade Secret #9

Get Through to Prospects: Bug 'Em

Be a pest, if necessary, to get a response from prospects.

Unreturned calls are not necessarily bad news. Imagine that your prospect has a hearing impairment, and that he or she simply might not have heard your call. Increase the volume, in effect, by continuing to call. Eventually either the prospect (or a secretary) will tell you to forget it, or, as frequently happens, you'll get an appointment.

•••

10 If You've Failed a Million Times...
...Try a Million and One Times

You fail at horseback riding as soon as you refuse to get up, dust yourself off, and remount one more time.
—AMERICAN COWBOY PROVERB

Persevering failures do not exist—they are simply people who have not yet succeeded. They are not failures. They have just failed—so far.

No matter how many times you strike out, you aren't a failure until you refuse to swing again. That is the moment you have failed.

But not until then.

While you are still swinging, you are still working toward success. Judging yourself by what others think of you gets you into dangerous territory. Judge yourself by what *you* think of you.

People who know how to persevere—even blindly or stubbornly—possess an incredibly important capability. If you have only blind perseverance, however, you have missed a crucial piece of the puzzle. Why you've missed that piece doesn't matter at all.

What *does* matter is that you recognize that something is missing from the way you do things, and that you get busy examining what's gone wrong in the past to get it right in the future.

Take the case of Sally, a woman I once hired to sell insurance. Despite being bright, aggressive, and knowledgeable, she never could really get her career off the ground. It didn't make sense, because I knew she was working hard to succeed. I decided to see if she was also *working smart.*

In analyzing her approach to selling life insurance, I discovered that she kept making the same "closing" technique mistake over and over again. Her problem was that she knew only one way to close.

We taught her closing techniques. She read Douglas Edward's *Closing the Sale,* one of the greatest books about the art of closing ever written. She very quickly realized that she couldn't close of-

23

ten with only one closing technique. Things began to change, and Sally became one of the most productive agents in my agency.

I hope that the ideas in this book will give you insight and help you find the puzzle piece that you are missing. Maybe that piece has always been close, but you just didn't recognize it. I hope that through this book we can figure out what that piece is and put it in place.

Are You Easily Discouraged?

If you are easily discouraged, you should know about the man

Who had less than one year of formal education.
Who was defeated when he ran for the Illinois legislature in '32.
Who bought a store in partnership in '33 and went into debt a few months later when the business failed.
Who did not receive nominations for Congress in '43 and '44.
Who took a seat in Congress in the House of Representatives in '47, but did not earn the reputation he hoped for.
Who did not run for a second term in '49 because he was so unpopular.
Who failed to get an appointment in '49 as commissioner of the General Land Office.
Who was denied election to the Senate in '55.
Who, still determined, ran for the Senate again and was defeated in '58.

That man was Abraham Lincoln!

••

Trade Secret #10

"Abe Lincoln's Our Most Satisfied Customer . . . "

Always come prepared with a list of appropriate personal references familiar to your prospect, preferably references in the same business or line of work as your prospect.

The best references are satisfied customers. They might also include people to whom you did not personally sell, but who have policies with your parent company.

••

11 *Mountain Climbing*

*A Madison Avenue advertising executive once noted that
50 percent of the ads he places brings in 90 percent of the
sales. "Unfortunately," he said, "I never know which half
until I run them."*

How can you identify and overcome the obstacles that you are
bound to encounter? I like to think about obstacles in concrete
terms—a mountain, a hurdle, a bridge—so that I can overcome
them more easily. For me there are mountains to climb daily.

I know to expect them.

When I get to them I'm not surprised, and I begin climbing in
the morning and there's no limit. I keep going. Every so often a
mountain is much higher than I thought it would be. Then it takes
a little more effort, and I have to climb harder. But every once in a
while the mountain is less than I thought it would be, and I jump
over it like nothing.

I always have plenty of time left over, so obstacles are nothing
more than temporary issues that have to be addressed, sur-
mounted, and abandoned. No mountain is too high.

None.

> ### *Some mountains you don't climb:*
> ### *You go around them instead!*

When I come to a mountain during the course of a day, I make
some instant decisions based on experience, environment, back-
ground, and what I think is possible. The worst that can happen is
that I make a wrong decision.

One theory that I use to make decisions is the "80/20/100/51"
rule.

The "80/20/100/51" rule is as follows: Most people in their lifetime spend 20 percent of their time gathering 80 percent of the
data about any given situation. When they have 80 percent of the
data, they feel it's not enough to make a decision. So they spend

the remaining 80 percent of their time trying to get the last 20 percent of the data. When they get that, they still think that they don't know enough.

The sales superstar, on the other hand, says, "When I've spent 20 percent of my time getting 80 percent of the data, I will make a decision 100 percent of the time and hope that I'm right 51 percent of the time."

In overcoming mountains you must gather and evaluate 80 percent of the facts in 20 percent of your time.

Look around. How high is the mountain?

Can you get around it?

Is there a path around it?

Can you get up halfway and go around?

Make it a point to get 80 percent of the facts in 20 percent of your time—then make a decision immediately. Go with it and you'll be right more than 51 percent of the time. In fact, *the fact is,* you'll probably be right more like 90 percent of the time because the processor in your head is able to put all the facts together for you. Forget about getting the last 20 percent; it won't help you anyway.

Take a chance.

••

Trade Secret #11

The 80/20/100/51 Rule

Immediately implement the 80/20/100/51 rule.

Identify one specific project, prospect, or activity that you have been stalling on because you think that you don't have all the information you need to proceed. You probably do have enough to get started now.

Make a decision and follow through immediately.

••

12 *You Can Learn To Do It Every Day*

Time goes you say? Ah, no! Alas, Time stays, we go.
—AUSTIN DOBSON

One of the most exciting things about the ideas in this book is that *they can all be learned.* Absolutely learned.

Successful selling is a learned discipline. It is not a science; it is an art. The knowledge is not restricted to only a few lucky people. It is available to you too.

You can learn the ideas of successful selling from this book and elsewhere. All that you need to do is make a conscious effort to learn. I am ready and willing to show you how.

> ## It's never too late to learn.

It is never—repeat *never*—too late to try to improve yourself and the way you sell. You can always do something to make yourself better.

I know people who have failed at six, seven, or eight different careers. One man was 50 years old before he began to practice the ideas in this book. Now he's 60. Last year, he earned almost $200,000 in life insurance commissions. It is never too late.

••

Trade Secret #12

Everybody Counts

Get to know the support staff at your office, and be sure to credit them—within and beyond their earshot—for the help they provide in the sales process. Make meticulous notes about their names, interests, and comments. In today's hustle and hassle world, when people realize that you remembered them and *that you had actually listened to what they were saying*—even in idle chit-chat—it makes a powerful, positive, and lasting impression.

••

13 *The Late Bloomer*

Know something. Know it well. Be known for knowing it.
—*ANONYMOUS*

A man named Mickey wanted to get into the life insurance business, so I agreed to discuss it with him. He was about 48 years old when we met.

"Sid," he said, "I don't know if I can do this. I may be over the hill."

Mickey had never made more than $40,000 or $50,000 a year in his life. Some may have seen that as a problem, but I saw it as a positive. Why?

Because had Mickey been making much more than that, he never would have thought about coming on board with us. He immediately fell in love with the business. He learned about the products, and he dedicated himself to learning about how to sell.

He loved meeting people, and he genuinely loved helping them. He knew that every time he wrote a policy, two important things happened. One, someone's life was substantially improved because of the insurance and as direct result of his work. And two, he made money.

Today he earns over $300,000 a year. It took him only two or three years to get to that level. He got motivated to succeed, and he's been doing it ever since. Mickey's a great turnaround story.

••

Trade Secret #13

Why People Succeed

The personal attributes listed below can very directly help you make money. Be alert to these success-producing characteristics. We all lack some of them. Determine which characteristics you don't have and work on developing them. They'll serve you well in all aspects of your life!

Sense of humor
Persistence

Stability
High energy
Goals
Outside interests
Expanding knowledge
Empathy
Respect for others
Forgiveness
High interest in work
Healthy self-image
Positive attitude

....

Trade Secret #14

Why People Fail

The personal characteristics listed below will cost you money!
Beware of these failure-creating characteristics. We all have some
of them. The trick is to identify those that you have, and to find a
way to resolve them favorably.

Self-preoccupation
Fear of responsibility
Lack of empathy
Closed mind
Poor ability to persuade others
Naive view of business
Poor imagination
Little flexibility
Inability to see total picture
Resentment toward authority
Laziness
Tendency to blame or criticize others

....

14 *When the Economy Is Weak, I'm at My Peak*

It's good to be king!
—MEL BROOKS in *History of the World, Part I*

When the economy goes bad, it is usually only in certain industries. Some sectors of the economy, like service groups, do outrageously well. Companies can capitalize on almost any adversity, like war or recession, and do fabulously.

I would say that three fourths of my current client population is doing wonderfully, and one fourth is doing badly. I don't pay too much attention to the one fourth—at least not now. They'll be in better shape soon enough.

I pay attention to the three fourths that are doing well.

Anybody coming into the life insurance business right now has an unparalleled opportunity because many agents are coasting through what they consider a slow time for the economy. They're saying, "Woe is me, I can't fix the world."

But their views are all cloudy. The people who are willing to work extra hard and do the things discussed in this book are going to clean up. While others are taking a nap, the intelligent, hardworking agents are eating their lunch.

We're proving this right now in our agency. Our business is booming. We can't handle the volume of applications coming in. Often I hear agents around the country crying about the state of things, and we can't handle the production. The only difference between them and us is that we know enough to work harder and smarter.

How? It's not magic, it's simple: We follow through more. We call on more people.

••

Trade Secret #15

Wake-up Call

This is the old story about the lion and the gazelle. It applies perfectly to the business of selling life insurance.

Every morning in Africa, a gazelle wakes up.

"I must run faster than the fastest lion, or I will be eaten."

Also every morning, a lion wakes up thinking a similar thought: "I must run faster than the slowest gazelle, or I will starve to death."

The moral?

It doesn't matter whether you are a lion or a gazelle, but when that sun comes up, you had better be off and running!

••

Part Two

Dreaming

15 Dream, Plan, Discipline
or, The Three-Part Process That Leads To Success

There are few better feelings in the world than having lined up a week's worth of appointments before lunch on Monday!

—ANONYMOUS

Successful people in all walks of business and personal life have certain similarities, patterns, and attitudes about the things they do and the way they do them. Once you identify what those things are, you'll be able to emulate those people and accomplish the same goals.

One of the central ideas to this book involves this three-part process: a dream, a plan, and discipline. You must have a dream, and the dream must be in color. If you can dream in color (and you *can* learn to), you've got the first step. Then at least you will know what you want. You must have a plan, and the plan is probably as important as the dream. If you don't know where you're going, and you haven't got a plan to get there, you won't arrive. The third part of the process is discipline, which is really like the motor on a boat. It makes the dream come true by executing the plan.

Trade Secret #16

Get Back to the Prospect on That

Action items—those that are on your "to do" list for a particular prospect—provide excellent opportunities to follow up. Upon wrapping up a meeting or a phone call, summarize the action items and offer to do some of them: "I'll take care of setting up the medical exam, and I'll call you to confirm it tomorrow," you might say. Usually, action items are things that must be accomplished sooner or later. By specifying what they are and by claiming ownership of the responsibility, you establish your role in the process, giving you credibility in the prospect's mind.

16 *Decide To Decide To Dream*

The most expensive possession you can have is a closed mind. It will cost you money all your life long.

—*Anonymous*

Before you can decide, you must decide to decide. Taking that step is part of your dream.

What is it, really, that you want?

Know what you want so clearly that you can see it, feel it, taste it. And when you get it, there will be no doubt in your mind that what you got was what you wanted. A clear vision of what you want will make deciding how to get there easier.

> ***Organize your dreams, and they'll organize you.***

Dreaming has to be very personal. Dreaming is goal setting. If you can dream, you can set goals.

No one says that money has to be important to you 24 hours a day, seven days a week. There is a time for everything.

Every day when you wake up, look at the urgent column of your "to do" list and put it in order according to priority. If writing an application is the number one priority for that day, then that is what you do first. Nothing else. If being home with your children that morning is your number one priority, then that's what you do. You do what's on your agenda.

You should organize what you have to do every day based on your overall plan. Then if you do the top five urgent things on your list, you will know that you have accomplished the five most important things in your life. Whatever they are, if you've done them, you've accomplished your day's work.

As you finish the "urgents" on your list, move the "importants" to the urgent column. Then as you finish the "importants," move the "everything elses" over. The goal is to accomplish the most important things first in your life.

....

Trade Secret #17

Get a Job!

Here's one way to get business owners thinking differently about annual premiums. Ask your prospect to put you on his or her payroll. Tell the prospect to imagine paying you by the hour. If the annual premium is $24,000, tell him or her that's like paying you $12.50 an hour, 40 hours a week. Mention that the janitor who cleans the prospect's building may be earning about that much. State that should the prospect die, you will bring in $1 million immediately to help keep the business going, to pay off any outstanding loans, to provide the spouse with an income without causing a drain on the company, and to help pay the huge estate taxes.

"Isn't that worth at least as much as the janitor who sweeps up around here?" you might ask.

Illustrate the costs to prospects as follows:

Annual Premium	Cost per Month	Cost per Hour
$24,000	$2,000	$12.50
$18,000	$1,500	$ 9.40
$12,000	$1,000	$ 6.25
$ 6,000	$ 500	$ 3.15

....

17 The Importance of Being a Dreamer
or How I Got My First Rolls Royce

Those who stand around saying this or that can't be done are usually interrupted by those who are doing it.

—ANONYMOUS

Dreaming puts your goal into perspective. You can't get what you want until you know what you want, whatever it may be.

Take me, for example. I had always wanted a Rolls Royce. I promised myself when I was a little kid, without knowing how to get it, that I was going to have a Rolls Royce before I was 40. At age 39, I wasn't broke; I was doing okay. But not Rolls Royce okay.

I wasn't Hall of Fame. I was still trying to get to the Hall of Fame, but I was just chopping wood every day. Every single day, trying hard.

I further fueled my dream with visits to a Rolls Royce dealership in New York.

"I have a very unusual request," I told the dealer. "I cannot afford to buy a Rolls Royce today but my nose is against your window like a little boy with a penny outside a candy store. Everything costs ten pennies, but I have only one penny. But I still want to buy one. If you will allow me to come in as often as I want, look at your cars, touch their leather, sit in them, do whatever I want, one day I'll buy a car from you."

The dealer looked at me like I was nuts.

"Mister," he said, "you do what you want. You're crazy. Go do what you want, but don't scare the sane customers away. And by all means, keep away from me."

I began visiting the showroom regularly.

I was always dressed up, so the dealer knew I wasn't going to hurt his cars. I drove to the dealership from Philadelphia one Saturday each month for 13 months. I sat in the car I wanted for three or four hours each time, touching and feeling, holding the steering wheel, sitting in the back and front seats, and opening the trunk. Some people suspected that I was crazy. But I knew the truth. I *was* crazy.

Well, I bought my first Rolls Royce in the fourteenth month. I saved enough money in those 13 months to do it. By having the dream so clear—I actually felt the dream—I found the money and I bought the car. For cash.

I was 39 years old. I bought the car before March of that year because I was going to be 40, and I had to have the car before then.

The power of a dream can be awfully strong—if you dream in detail about what you really want. That's what happened to me. And that was only one dream.

Now, what does that mean to anybody else?

It doesn't matter what the dream is, but first you have to establish it. For me, it was to have a Rolls Royce before I was 40. That was just the dream then. It might have been a new home, it might have been to find a prospect who could buy a million dollar policy.

Your dreams must be very vivid, very real, very true for you. Whatever your mind can conceive, you can accomplish.

••

Trade Secret #18

Sticks and Stones

When a prospect makes a hostile, nasty, or aggressive remark, look for the source of his or her anxiety—there may be a sales opportunity there.

For example, suppose the prospect says, "Your prices are much too high for me. I'm not interested."

Diffuse the question by asking another like, "Well, what do you think a person your age should be paying?"

Whenever you get into trouble, ask a probing, open-ended question. Beginning a question with the words *who, what, when, why,* or *how* ensures that the question cannot be answered with a yes or no.

Also, never respond defensively.

••

18 *You and Your Dream Are Unique*

Never, ever, accept a no from anyone—especially from yourself!

—SIDNEY FRIEDMAN

Everybody is genuinely unique. This means you too.

The dream is totally different for everybody; whatever a person wants to accomplish counts as that person's dream. All you need do is make sure that you've given some time to your dream.

It's been said that most people spend more time planning their two-week summer vacation than they do the entire year's worth of work, and I believe it.

I wonder sometimes how much time most sales people give to planning the whole picture. They may plan for a particular sale, event, or day in their lives, but they don't plan the big picture.

It is every bit as important—perhaps more important—to plan the decade as it is to plan the afternoon, the week, or the month. You have to plan ahead.

Either you're willing to keep to your plan or you're not. If you don't know where you are going, as Yogi Berra says, you'll wind up somewhere else.

He's right.

So how am I different in my approach to sales and management? How am I unique? Let me give you some specific details about my own personal approach to life and to life insurance:

- I am different in that I do not accept mediocrity. Sure, you have heard this before. But how many people do you know who actually act upon it, ridding their lives of negative people and of those who refuse to believe?
- I am different in that I care about my clients. Another cliché you say? Absolutely not. People are what life means to me, and I am willing to make any type of sacrifice to maintain, cement, or build relationships.
- I am different in that I don't really like the insurance business. It's true. I *love* the insurance business. I am amazed at how many of my colleagues apologize for their industry. You know

40

what I am talking about. They say they are in marketing, instead of sales. Or they say they are in the insurance business
without mentioning sales. I love to tell people what I do and
how well I do it.

- I am different in that I live to work and not work to live. There
  is no line between work and play for me. I have eight telephone numbers that I give to clients—three of which ring directly into my home. My children and wife have taken active
  roles in helping to build my business. My work is so inter-
  twined with my life that one is not separate from the other.
  And I like it that way.

- I am different in that I know how to act. Let's face it, ideas are
  cheap. I can sit down and spew forth ideas for hours at a time.
  *But it's the implementation of those ideas that make things
  happen.* I know how to motivate myself and motivate others to
  act.

- I am different in that integrity is more important than a sale. It's
  amazing how often people will sacrifice what's right for what's
  profitable. But you know what? In the long run, what is right is
  also profitable. Many times throughout my career, I have traded
  a quick commission for the good of the client. Nine times out
  of ten, that sacrifice comes back to me in future sales and commissions. And if it doesn't? So what. I'm still way ahead, as I
  see it.

- I am different in that I am money-motivated. Most people say
  they are, but they are not. Most people are motivated by the
  course of least resistance. They avoid what is difficult and un-
  pleasant, no matter how profitable it might be.

- I am different in that I have been married to the same woman
  for 27 years. To some, that labels me as being crazy. But not if
  you know my wife. Sue has been a pillar of strength to me
  throughout my career. Our relationship is proof of our integrity and ability to build long-term relationships.

- I am different in that I am a skilled actor. Sales is acting. You
  have to know how to play the role that your clients expect—
  while still being honest with them. Actors can persuade and
  convince. Actors can portray the realities of a situation with
  such honesty that they move people to respond through
  action.

- I am different in that I am creative. Most salespeople's idea of creativity is the message that goes on the holiday cards to clients. My creativity strikes at the heart of sales—it's focused on building relationships, improving presentations, and closing a sale.
- I am different in that I never listened to a negative. That's a pretty powerful statement. But it's true. I ignore people who say "it can't be done," "there's no way," or "it's impossible." If I had, I never would have become one of the nation's most productive insurance salespeople and the owner of four successful businesses.

Have you had enough?

Believe me, I could go on and on. But I think you get the idea, which is this: To be super successful in insurance sales—or any type of sales—you have to distinguish yourself.

••

Trade Secret #19

Invent Yourself

Find a personal trademark that will distinguish you from others. It could be your personality, your letterhead, your commitment to service, your depth of knowledge, or the way you dress. Anything that distinguishes you from the crowd.

Select it carefully.

And then invest in it. Do everything you can to promote that image. Clorox bleach contains the same chemical as other bleaches, but it is probably the only brand name you know. Its manufacturers invested in distinguishing it from the others.

••

Part Three

Planning

19 *Plan Your Plan*

You may be disappointed if you fail, but you are doomed if you don't try.

—BEVERLY SILLS

You must plan your plan very carefully, since it is equally important as the dream. Once you have all your wonderful ideas, you must decide what *specifically* you are going to do to make your dream come true.

A map tells how to get from here to there. There's no better way to get from here to there than a straight line. When a straight line isn't available, you must outline the best alternative. Unfortunately, life doesn't offer us many perfectly straight lines, so, after much trial and error, we've come to rely on our reason to make plans.

You have to know when to start, how long it will take, what you are trying to accomplish, and what checkpoints are along the way. Simply, you have to make a plan to get where you want to go.

If your goal is to make Round Table, that means earning $4,166 in commissions each month, or about $1,040 each week. If each application brings in about $500 in commission, then you do two apps a week. It takes two apps a week, eight apps a month to make Round Table. Do you have eight apps for the month? Do you have $4,166? If you don't, you have missed the target.

You must ask yourself what you must do to get those eight apps. How many closing interviews will it take? How many telephone calls must you make? How many referrals must you get to get $4,166 a month?

That's the bottom line.

Plan for the Unexpected

When the unexpected knocks you off course, get back on course immediately. Identify the obstacle. If it's a mountain, go around it. But don't shrink away from the unexpected problem. Attack it.

••

Trade Secret #20

Urgent, Important, and Everything Else

Make a list with three columns titled "urgent," "important," and "everything else." Use the list to give priority to tasks or events.

Think of it as *your* list, not your manager's, not your spouse's, not your mortgage company's. Nobody should have any input but you. Use the list daily to categorize everything that is in your mind and in your plan.

You must label what—in your opinion—is "urgent" for each day. For example, if you think that your family fits the "urgent" category for that day, put them in your urgent column. If writing a life insurance policy is only "important," put it in that column. But if writing a life insurance policy is "urgent," then put it in the "urgent" column.

"Urgent," "important," and "everything else."

It's nobody's agenda but yours. It will help you to keep focused and free your thoughts because you'll be confident that you're working on the most important tasks each day.

••

Trade Secret #21

Close to You

Create a specific, written list of your goals and how you'll achieve them in the coming time period. It doesn't matter if that period is a day, a week, a month, a quarter, or the entire year. What *does* matter is that you create the plan and keep it nearby.

The plan should fit on one side of a plain piece of typing paper. Make copies of it and keep one at home, at the office, and in your briefcase. Then your plan will become second nature to you.

••

20 The Four-Step Goal-Planning Process

Act quickly, think slowly.

—GREEK PROVERB

Some things in life don't require complete understanding, like how a car engine works or how telephone connections are made. It doesn't really matter to us how some things happen, as long as they happen when we want them to.

But the goal-planning process is definitely different. If you're going to plan a goal, and if you intend to work at it until you've reached it, then you must understand the *process*. Understanding how it works is critical because you and your habits, behavior, and thoughts all become part of the process. The process is totally unique to *you,* but generally it includes answering four questions.

- Where are you now?
- Where do you want to go?
- How will you get there?
- What are the checkpoints along the way to make sure you are on track?

Let's take each question one step at a time.

Step One: Where Are You Now?

What have you done up until now?

Make a list of things that you've accomplished that you like, and another of the things that you don't like. Evaluate the list. Conduct an asset inventory of what you've accomplished to date and decide what you're happy or unhappy about.

Step Two: Where Do You Want To Go?

To decide where you want to go, you must develop a road map of what you didn't like on previous trips and also of what you need to do to avoid the same mistakes. Or if you do like where you've been heading, decide how to continue going in the right direction.

Decide what you want based on where you are now and where you want to go. You might say, Okay, I've accomplished *A, B* and *C.* I need to accomplish *D, E,* and *F.* I want to do it in *X* years.

Start putting the goals down on paper. Write specific things like, "In five years I want to have a house," or, "I'd like to have a second child," or, "I'd like to make some more money."

Step Three: How Will You Get There?

Once you have determined where you are and where you want to go, you need to work on the hardest part of the road map: How are you going to get there?

You can't simply wake up one morning and decide to start doing things and hope that you'll reach your goals. You'll get lost so fast your head will spin. You won't know where you're going, and you'll wind up somewhere else. Believe me, detours, distractions, and obstacles are abundant. They've tripped me up plenty of times.

You might have a good analysis of where you are and a strong desire to go somewhere, but unless you have an intelligent and specific plan to get there, you're not going to make it. Your plan is the road map. If you follow that map, even if you encounter detours or get delayed you *will* get where you want to go.

Step Four: What Are the Checkpoints Along the Way?

There are checkpoints everywhere in life. When you veer off course by eating too much and exercising too little, your clothes act as a checkpoint: They become too tight and uncomfortable. When you exceed the speed limit, a cop with a radar gun will be happy to issue you a checkpoint: a ticket that results in a fine and points against your driver's license. When you spend more money than you have in your checking account, the bank sends you a little checkpoint: a bounced check notice.

In your plan, you have to determine the checkpoints yourself. This is part of working harder because creating workable checkpoints is hard. You have to calculate, evaluate, and analyze. If you say you're going to make $40,000 in commissions this year that's about $3,335 each month. You have to know where you are, where you are going, and how you are going to get there. Then you have to figure out a reasonable way to measure your progress.

It isn't easy, but it pays great.

••

Trade Secret #22

Do Research on Your Prospects

Answer the following questions before you leap into an appointment:

- Who will be there?
- How many people will be there?
- What do they expect from you?
- What is their experience in the past?
- When was their program last reviewed?
- Is there competition?
- Who will make the decision to buy?

••

21 *Create Effective Checkpoints*

Slight not what's near through aiming at what's far.
—EURIPIDES

As you develop your checkpoints, you'll have to be sure they are effective. Then you must enforce them and correct problems that cause you to miss checkpoints. Once you learn to create checkpoints and apply them to your plan, you will develop great confidence that lets you forge ahead without distraction because you know that periodically you'll be checking in to see how you are doing.

If you are driving from Seattle to New Orleans along a superhighway, for example, you don't need to waste time reading every single sign on the road. Your map gives you the checkpoints: Oregon, Idaho, Wyoming, and so on. It keeps you going in the right direction. You can relax, confident that you are on schedule and going in the right direction.

Once you get to Louisiana, the map gets more specific: Jefferson Parish, Bourbon Street, and so on. Finally, you reach your hotel.

If you set your goals and measure your progress, you'll reach your destination in good time.

> ### Bad checkpoints can be more trouble than no checkpoints at all.

You can get on an airplane that's going 600 miles per hour and it's wonderful because you're going really fast. Except for one serious problem. Your checkpoint warned you to make sure that you took a specific airline. Unfortunately, you didn't plan it specifically enough. You find yourself on the wrong airline traveling to Juno, instead of Jasper.

That's worse than just staying home and watching the tube.

In other words, be very careful when you set your life insurance sales goals. You could be doing a great job and heading somewhere fast but you'd better be going in the right direction. Well-crafted checkpoints will make sure you get there.

So, again, if you know where you are now (through self-analysis), know where you want to go (your hopes and dreams), and if you develop a plan (the road map), begin the journey and don't stop. With checkpoints along the way, you'll achieve your goals.

••

Trade Secret #23

Jot That Down

Post-call evaluations are important, especially with new prospects, because the day's distractions make it easy to forget conversations.

I recommend salespeople create a form that they can review *as soon as possible after ending a meeting or phone call*—in the car, train, or anywhere—so that the details of the meeting are still fresh in mind.

Questions to ask yourself include:

- What are the prospect's problems?
- Did I create a credible relationship?
- What follow-up activities are needed to move this case along?
- Did I ask for the business?

••

22 *Discipline Yourself*

Success is attained by sacrificing other choices along the way.

—ANONYMOUS

Part of you wants to eat the whole pizza, but another part of you wisely says, Have one slice, eat it slowly, savor the flavor, and that's it. You don't need the whole pizza.

Since the beginning of history, religious scholars, philosophers, and psychologists have argued about those two opposing forces within human beings. We are not going to resolve that monumental issue in this book, but we can take a few cues from that ageless debate: Don't give in to the easy way.

Set goals that you have to stretch to reach. Like the popular saying, your reach should exceed your grasp.

Larry Wilson, formerly of the Wilson Learning Corporation, defined professionals as having three qualities: They're good and they know it; they keep getting better; and they critique their own performance. Wilson says that if you do those three things, you will create a positive self-image because, in fact, you will be good. You'll be a professional.

The better you do, the better you feel, and the better you feel, the better you do. I think you have to look at your self-image, the way you look in the mirror.

Wilson also describes professionals as being conscious competents. A conscious competent is someone who is good and knows it. Sometimes we're *unconscious* competents: We're good but we don't know why. We strive to become conscious competents: We're good and we do know why.

Other times we're conscious *incompetents:* We know we can do it better, so we keep trying to get better. And, unfortunately, sometimes we're unconscious incompetents: We're bad and we don't even know we're bad.

You've got to keep striving to be better.

Be good and know it, keep getting better, and critique your own performance. If you do these three things, your self-image will be good. You have said to yourself, "I'm going to get better. I'm not going to give up. I'm going to keep getting better and better until I'm perfect."

You may never get there, but the journey is wonderful.

••

Trade Secret #24

How Discipline Leads to Success

- You've got to have discipline to keep going when things get tough.
- You can turn failure into success by having the discipline to get better. Just think of this formula:

   Failure + Discipline = Success
- Part of being disciplined is having the will to try more. You'll lose more, but you'll win more, too. Here's another formula for success to remember:

   Try more = Lose More + Win More
- Always be ready.
- Do what others do—just do more of it.
- Be committed, persist, and your discipline will see you through.

   Remember these three keys which you need for success:

Discipline
Persistence
Commitment

Remind yourself again and again that you need these for your success.

••

Part Four

Get Started

23 *Time Management*

Your most important personal asset is your ability to get up in the morning and go to work. People need to insure that asset.

—*Anonymous*

Never shut the machine down; the management of time is crucial.

The whole sales process works only if it keeps moving from step to step. Certainly, many things can get in the way of managing your time: crises that come up, unexpected telephone calls, clients who need to see you "Now!"

Breaks in the sales process shouldn't break your overall strategy for time management. You've got to live by a clock—if you promise yourself you'll do something, you must find a way to get it done. Don't break the system down. Managing your time takes a great deal of effort, but the results are worth it.

The only way you can get to the successful completion of your plan—and your dream—is with proper time management which means having the discipline to do what you said you would do. Do not underestimate the importance of this point.

Will you do in the morning what you promised yourself the night before? Winners do it in the morning. Losers think about it sometime the following afternoon.

Also remember that if you're not the lead dog, the view never changes. You've got to be first.

You've got to get up earlier and do more.

Accomplish more.

••

Trade Secret #25

Demonstrating Immediate Action

Make a call from the customer's office or home, if appropriate, and insist that someone at your office get on your request immediately: "Larry, it is absolutely urgent to get that information out of the computer and call me back here at 144-3944. Mr. Jenkins needs to know right away!"

This technique demonstrates to the prospect that you are taking his or her needs seriously.

•••

24 *Hearing No Is the Starting Point*

Good people are good because they've come to wisdom through failure.

—WILLIAM SAROYAN

The old sales adage applies here: The more *no*'s you get, the closer you are to the *yes*. You have to keep getting *no*'s.

If you don't get any *no*'s, it means you're not seeing anybody. If you see people, some are bound to say no.

A *lot* of people are going to say no to you.

They don't like your hair.

They don't like the way you dress.

They don't like the color of your skin.

They don't like your policy.

They don't like your presentation.

They don't like your personality.

Somebody's not going to like you. Wait a minute. *A lot of people aren't going to like you.* Get used to it.

I'm saying they'll probably not like you nine times out of ten. They may not literally dislike you, but basically you're going to get *no*'s. The *no*'s will make you stronger to go for that one *yes* you're after every day.

Go Ahead, Make My Day: Say No

To tell you the truth, I don't really feel comfortable with a prospect until he or she says that magic word: No!

That's the starting point, the gun going off.

Nothing happens until the prospect says no. When a prospect says no, then you are in business! If he or she doesn't say anything—if you don't get any reaction to what you are saying—face it, you're making a speech. If you get a reaction, even negative, at least you're having dialogue. That is what you want to happen.

Unless you're running for governor, speeches are bad news. No is part of dialogue. It gives you a chance to find out what's the matter.

How can I fix it? Ask yourself. There's got to be a reason why the person said no.

Most people don't say no for the sake of saying it; they say it for a valid reason. Some people say no because they don't fully understand you, so you have to be a bit more clear. Find out what they want. Dig deeper. A great trade secret is to do more discovery. Find out why they're saying no, and you'll have a chance to overcome it and offer them what they want.

Once you have a better offer you have a chance to win. Then the dialogue becomes a win/win situation.

But you have to hear no nine times to hear one yes.

Sometimes I think you *have* to hear no nine times to hear one yes. I sometimes wonder if that rule is even in the physics books, sandwiched somewhere between inertia and gravity.

•••

Trade Secret #26

Raising the Stakes

Upping the ante—meeting with someone from a higher level of management in your prospect's company—can often be accomplished by bringing in someone from a higher level of management from your company. Or, bring along an expert. If the prospect's situation requires you to seek out the advice of an expert on a particular subject, get one, even if it means sharing the commission.

Remember, 50 percent of the commission is a lot more than 100 percent of nothing.

•••

Trade Secret #27

Converting a "No Action" Response

Only five reasons account for a "no action" response from a prospect.

1. The problem with his or her current policy—if there is one—is not clear.
2. The solution is not clear.
3. The prospect thinks that he or she can't afford the solution.

4. The prospect is not concerned about the problem.
5. The prospect has no confidence in the agent.

Congratulations!
You can control every one of these reasons.

• •

25 *Quitting Time?*

For every minute you spend regretting a sale that did not happen, you lose 60 seconds of trying again.

—ANONYMOUS

In the old days, I would generally quit before I finished a day's work. I'd do all the things that were on my calendar, but I wouldn't do a thing more. When I started doing just one extra task a day—one more phone call, one more appointment, one more letter—that extra effort seemed to work.

Suddenly the small extra effort had a very marked effect.

I made one more sales call every day, even though I didn't want to talk anymore. I was tired and wanted to go home. I learned to do it then, and I still do it now. I'll go on working when everyone else quits. I'll spend that extra few more minutes to get results.

I make working a little longer a game that I play. As soon as I've reached the point when I've had enough and want to go home, I do just one more thing. Whenever I feel that I've had it for the day, whenever I tell myself that I've done enough, I play the game.

When I'm tired and I want to leave, I challenge myself to make one more phone call. When I'm exhausted and I'm going home, I challenge myself to make one more stop on the way.

I also play the game at other times of the day when I don't feel like working. If I want to get something done in the morning, I'll make the appointment for 6:45 instead of 7:30. I may want to stay in bed, but I get up and do what I have to do. Sometimes, I get home late, at 10 or 11 o'clock, but the next morning I'm up at 5 o'clock. At times I feel like I just take naps every night instead of sleeping.

But to me, the game is worth it.

Trade Secret #28

Call It Paycheck Insurance

Present disability income insurance as a way to insure a prospect's paycheck: "Do you have the regular type of disability in-

62

come insurance that only waives your life insurance premiums, or do you have the comprehensive type that waives your life insurance premiums *and* pays you an income for life?'' If you knew you were going to have a coronary tonight, would you buy this plan today?''

••

Trade Secret #29

Home Sweet Home...in a Minute

When you are ready to quit for the day, try staying in your office for an extra 15 minutes. Something good will come of it. Make a few more phone calls. Forget about *just* working smarter. It is a dangerous myth. Do something today that qualifies as working harder *and* smarter!

••

26 Sooner or Later . . .

What I hear, I may forget. What I see, I may remember.
What I do, I understand.

—*ANONYMOUS*

I wasn't always convinced I could be successful. I did terribly in high school. I probably never would have graduated if the dean hadn't liked the way I played trumpet. I thought I was never going to make it.

I got into New York University only because of my mother. She pushed and annoyed the dean until he let me in. (Maybe I got some of my persistence from her!) I was thrown out of college after three or four months. Mom pleaded with them again and I got back in school.

But it was then that I decided to try something else. I tried it—life insurance, of course—and it worked. I didn't give up on myself. I kept trying and trying, and it wasn't too late. I found what worked.

At 30 years old it's easy to think your whole life is molded. Well, I've seen 50-year-olds come into business and be huge successes when before that they had been failing.

I've been training agents for 25 years. I would say that I've put 300 agents through the system. I've hired people who were inexperienced and others who were already somewhat successful. Of those 300 agents, about 250 failed miserably.

That may not be good, but it is understandable. About 30 or 40 of them had some degree of success, and probably 10 or 20 had a great degree of success—to the point where they consistently made Round Table, Top of the Table, or Court of the Table.

I can think of at least a half dozen of those who came into the business over age 50. They decided that they wanted more from life. They got into the insurance business, applied some discipline to their lives, and suddenly things took off. Some of them are still with me after ten years. They're still here working hard and breaking records.

It's never too late.

I like to believe that their joining the insurance business truly changed their lives. The insurance business provided the opportunity, and they took advantage of it. It made all the difference for them.

It can for you too.

••

Trade Secret #30

The Double-Duty Buy-Sell

Instead of the principals buying insurance on each other in the typical cross-purchase method, two principals have their spouses buy the insurance on the executives. Upon the death of executive A, executive A's spouse makes the insurance proceeds available to the corporation as a loan.

Example: Assume the amount loaned is $100,000. The corporation has an obligation to do two things: first, to pay back the $100,000 loan, and second, to pay off the buy-sell agreement, also in the amount of $100,000.

Procedure: Upon the death of executive A, the surviving spouse gets the $100,000 from the insurance company, and lends it to the corporation. The corporation agrees to pay interest at an agreed current rate by note. If the corporation pays back the $100,000 for the buy-sell agreement, executive A's spouse still is due $100,000 for the loan. The corporation agrees to pay it back in ten equal installments of $10,000 each for ten years, but they also owe interest on a level basis of 10 percent. Therefore, the spouse gets $10,000 of principal and $10,000 in interest for a total of $20,000 for each of the 10 years.

Result: The surviving spouse gets $100,000 down payment treated as the buy-sell and $20,000 a year over the next ten years, or $200,000, as repayment of the loan. In total, the spouse receives $300,000 for a $100,000 interest. In effect, that is a double-duty—or even triple-duty—buy-sell agreement. What do you think?

••

27 *Getting Started Is More Important than Creativity*

It isn't that they can't see the solution. It is that they can't see the problem!

—G.K. CHESTERTON

Creativity is important, but your ability to apply what you have learned is more important. Knowledge has to be applied *creatively.* Most people spend 80 percent of their time trying to find the most creative way to climb the mountain.

I say, begin climbing it now, or just go around it. You'll acquire and process data as you go along and your path will become clearer. Decisions will come by keeping your eyes and ears open; they will be based on experience, not speculation.

Douglas Edwards, perhaps one of the best sales trainers on the subject of closing, often was asked when the best time to close is.

"Close too soon, and too often, and you'll learn when to close," was his answer.

The same applies here. Climb the wrong mountains too many times. Climb the right ones too fast. Make some mistakes—that's the way to learn.

Just keep doing it.

You'll get over or around the mountains. Some of the mountains you won't need to climb, you can go around them easily. But don't get off the mountain. That's the most important issue. If you do it wrong, so what? You'll do it right 51 percent of the time, and you learn so much from the other 49 percent that it is worth the time.

Please don't misunderstand me.

I'm not suggesting that a creative approach to solving problems is not important. It is. Most people wind up copying somebody else. Creativity is *very* important. But it's more important to get started.

Even if you don't have the most creative approach, you'll become more creative as you go along. As you get more information, let your creativity take over. Understand the creative process, and you'll learn to solve problems more quickly. You'll turn the axe sharp side down, as my father said.

Part of creativity is finding out what the crowd is doing wrong. *Then don't do it.* Choose your own path. If the crowd is doing it vanilla, you must do it pistachio. You've got to have some creativity.

Just don't forget to push the start button and get started.

Some Specific Ideas for Getting Started

For some reason, some people just get stuck.

If you are one of those people who is having trouble actually getting off the ground, relax: I have collected 19 of the simplest, most direct, and to-the-point sales ideas for *specific* life and health insurance products right here, for you to use *immediately.*

Refer to any of the following ideas *right now,* and you will find that you are off and running!

••

Trade Secret #31

Universal Life Selling Technique

A great way to sell universal life insurance is to show the guaranteed rates that the company has and, whatever the rate the company is presently quoting, subtract one hundred basis points thus reducing the chances for any lawsuits in the future.

••

Trade Secret #32

Term Life Selling Technique

Use a spreadsheet program that shows eight companies' term products on one page to sell term life insurance. This way, the prospect can pick the one he or she wants from you.

••

Trade Secret #33

Whole Life Selling Technique

A great way to sell whole life insurance is to compare it to term life insurance. Use a computer program that compares them based on a given rate of interest. You'll find that whole life, with its tax-free status, often beats anything on the market.

••

Trade Secret #34

Buy-out Insurance Selling Technique

Don't forget to sell buy-out insurance. When someone has a buy-sell agreement funded by life insurance, make sure it is also funded by disability insurance.

••

Trade Secret #35

Deferred Compensation Selling Technique

A great way to sell a deferred compensation policy is to show it as a private pension plan offered to employees on an after-tax basis. The growth is tax free.

••

Trade Secret #36

Payroll Deduction Plan Selling Technique

A great way to sell a payroll deduction plan is to write a group insurance case in which you control the group with Blue Cross, Blue Shield, or another insurance company in your city. Add payroll deduction to it so that you can use not only the company checkbook but employee paychecks as well to get premium money.

••

Trade Secret #37

Another Payroll Deduction Plan Selling Technique

Another great way to sell a payroll deduction plan is with a flexible benefit plan. With these plans, the cost for health insurance is deducted before taxes, so the employee pays taxes on a lower amount.

Then the employee can use the savings to buy more insurance.

• •

Trade Secret #38

Selling Company Pensions and Profit-Sharing Plans

Get managers to see that company pensions and profit-sharing plans are investments in the future, rather than payments to Uncle Sam.

• •

Trade Secret #39

Split-Dollar Selling Technique

A good opportunity to sell a split-dollar policy is when you have a person with a great need but no money and another entity like a corporation with no need but a lot of money and a desire to help a key executive buy a policy. If a corporation buys a policy for a key executive, all of the corporation's money is guaranteed back regardless of whether the employee lives, dies, quits, or becomes disabled.

• •

Trade Secret #40

Estate Planning Technique

A great way to sell estate planning is to find people having estates of $2 million or more. They have a 55 percent tax lien on their estate, and need estate planning to make the most of their money. It's surprising how often people with substantial estates do little or no estate planning.

• •

Trade Secret #41

Group Health Insurance Technique

One way to sell group health insurance is to learn whether enough employees are unhappy with their current group health insurance program. If they are, use that information to get a face-to-face meeting with that company's decision maker.

••

Trade Secret #42

Key Employee Selling Technique

A great way to sell key employee insurance is to pay close attention to a manager's comments about employees who are valuable, and then suggest the manager insure them for at least one...or two years' profit in the event that the key person dies or is disabled.

The boss may be the key employee in the company. If so, suggest insuring one or two years' company profits in the event that he or she dies.

••

Trade Secret #43

Annuities Selling Technique

One way to sell annuities is to find people who are currently buying certificates of deposit (CDs). CDs are taxable today, whereas annuities are taxable in the future. The entire growth is tax-deferred with annuities.

••

Trade Secret #44

Flexible Benefit Plan Selling Technique

A great way to sell flexible benefit plans is to find companies that are currently deducting health insurance costs from employee paychecks, or those that want to show employees how to spend their benefit dollars any way they wish, like with a comprehensive, cafeteria plan.

••

Trade Secret #45

Long-Term Care Selling Technique

Use the concept of financial independence to sell long-term care insurance. A prospect with a strong desire not to be dependent on others when they reach age 65 will likely be interested.

Trade Secret #46

Disability Income Selling Technique

A great way to sell disability income insurance is to show statistics on deaths and disabilities for different age groups.

Trade Secret #47

Group Life Insurance Selling Technique

Identifying companies that have life insurance and discovering how to make it better, cheaper, or both is a good technique for selling group life insurance.

In doing so, you can develop contacts in that company's human resources department, and that relationship can give you access to other life insurance sales opportunities.

Trade Secret #48

Group Disability Income Selling Technique

A great way to sell group disability income insurance is to describe how someone in a similar company was disabled. Take the time to find out about such cases. Your company's claims department is a good place to start.

If you can't find a report about a disabled employee in a similar company, find one about someone in a nearby company.

Tell your prospect how the disability coverage not only helped the disabled employee, but how it also contributed to higher company morale because other employees felt secure with their coverage.

Remember, in relating anecdotes about other people or companies, take care to protect privacy.

You can describe general situations, but never say anything that leads to the identification of a particular person.

••

Trade Secret #49

Selling Disability Insurance to a Reluctant Prospect

Relate the following scenario to your prospect: Imagine that you have two job offers. Job A pays you $60,000 annually, with standard medical benefits. Job B pays you $58,000 annually, with standard medical benefits, *plus a guaranteed income of $3,000 each month until you are 65, in the event that you become ill or injured and cannot work.* Which job would you prefer, Job A or Job B?

(Thanks, by the way, to Irwin "Burt" Meisel of Detroit for this sales idea.)

••

28 *Simple Ideas Create Powerful Changes*

If you are not the leader of the pack, the view never changes.

—*ANONYMOUS*

Planning and dreaming are, of course, critically important parts of the success process. But sooner or later, you'll have to put those ideas, thoughts, plans, dreams, and hopes to work for you. You do that by *getting started!*

I planned this book for a long time. What would I say, how would I say it? When I finally sat down at my computer to write, I began to worry that some life insurance salespeople might find it too simple.

Why did I worry about that?

Because I realized that if you wanted to see success through Sidney Friedman's eyes, the rules were going to be simple, short, and sweet. And they would be repeated frequently because they work.

These simple rules, which have helped me so much on the journey to success, can be learned. But, more importantly, they have to be believed. These ideas will put money in your pocket, but only if you implement them. It's up to you to get started. Even if you are an idiot and chop wood with the dull side of the axe blade, you'll still get somewhere. You'll still make progress and learn.

You have to learn the rules, and, just as importantly, you have to come to believe that they will work. Only then will they work.

The rules will work for you, but they won't *do* the work for you. That is up to you. You have to start and you have to keep going all the time.

That's it, really.

You have to be in the right place and go in the right direction. As far as I'm concerned, in order to succeed, you have no choice but to never let up.

Then you cannot miss.

People often fail because they stop priming the pump. You must pump and pump even though no water is coming out of the pump. You must keep pumping. If you stop the moment before the water spurts out, you'll never see it, even though you were only seconds away from getting what you wanted. You have to keep pumping until you get the results you desire.

Simple determination has helped me through many times. I have learned that no matter what the problem is, I'll eventually have it solved if I stay at it long enough.

Time after time I tell myself—and I keep playing this game—that I don't want to stop until I have the problem solved, so I work a little harder and dig a little deeper. I tell myself that if I stay at it a little longer, I'll find the answer.

For example, when I lose something—like a book I'm reading—I ask myself Where did I put it? Where did it go? I can't find it, and I tear the house apart. Instead of giving up and assuming it's gone or that someone threw it out, I look one more time. If I still don't find it, I say to myself, I'm going to look for it again—even though I've been over every square inch of the place a hundred times!

Then do you know what happens?

I go right to the place where the book is. I can't explain why it works. It is simply the process.

It's like the old joke, "How come whenever I lose something, I always find it in the last place I look?" It's never in the next to the last place. Always the last place.

When do you finally make a sale? When the customer finally buys. Not before. It's happened in my life over and over again with clients who have said no to me and I decided to try one more time, just one more time.

What happens?

They say, "All right, come on over." Then I make a sale, but only because I called one more time.

But you have to be there when that happens. Only you can arrange for that to happen. It is all due to discipline and never letting up. It may be trite, but with me I try over and over again, and it works every time. I don't stop when everybody else does. You don't have to either.

The story of the tortoise and the hare applies to my life, but I put a twist on it, of course. I like to be a tortoise in hare's clothing, and generally I conduct my life that way. People look at me and think I am like a hare, running around crazily and at top speed all the time.

I'm always in action, always moving. I appear to have only two speeds—frantic and stop. Yet I really am a tortoise. I go methodically. I cross the finish line every time. I may be slower than most, but I always get across the line.

A lot of people run faster than me and pass me, but I'll catch them at the end and cross the line first.

The world—and especially the life insurance business—is full of hares.

Sometimes I try to disguise the fact that I'm more like a tortoise than a hare. I feel pressure to act like all the hares. But I've learned that it's more important to be proud of being unique. Besides, I've seen a lot of tortoises running circles around those who appear to be hares.

I've also seen a lot of hares trying to be like tortoises. But the hares, with their quick starts and fast sprints, don't have a chance in the world of ever reaching the finish line.

Never.

•••

Trade Secret #50

Too Late

A recent court decision has shown it's too late to adopt a wage continuation plan once a key person has been disabled.

Tell a prospect about this case. You might relate the case hypothetically by choosing a real name, like "Mr. Sanford," so prospects identify with the person.

A Mr. Sanford was president of a company. He had a heart ailment which gradually grew more serious. Sanford was generally confined to his home, but he continued to serve as president until the year of his death. During his illness, the company continued to pay his annual salary.

The court found that because there was no sick pay plan, the company could not deduct the salary payments to Sanford as a business expense. The company had to pay back taxes and interest to the IRS. The taxes and penalties were assessed against the estate for the income Sanford had received.

••

Trade Secret #51

The "KISS" Formula

I'm a great fan of "KISSing." KISSing stands for Keep It Simple, Sweetheart.

For example, when showing a prospect an idea, try to keep it simple. Usually, I draw only two columns: "you pay" and "you get." If I'm with someone who is more knowledgeable, then I'll add a third column: "cash equity."

Most of the time, however, it's good to stick to two columns. Insurance can be quite complicated, but it must be presented in a very simple, direct way.

••

Trade Secret #52

Help Prospects Remember

Studies have shown that memory is better when messages are received by more than one sense.

	Amount of Message Retained	
Senses Receiving Message	Next day	After one week
Hearing only	10%	Under 1%
Sight only	30%	Under 5%
Hearing, sight, and touch	50%	10%

Get prospects involved in what you are discussing by stimulating their senses.

••

29 *When You Get a Brainstorm, Lock It Up*

> *Life insurance is the most amazing product in the world. It creates wealth—by the stroke of a pen—where there once was none.*
>
> —SIDNEY FRIEDMAN

Capture your brainstorms. They are gifts from nature.

The most important thing to remember about a brainstorm is to write everything down immediately. Don't trust your memory. Your brain may work like a computer, but the recall is only as good as the way you store the data.

I recommend that you keep a little book in your pocket, and every time an idea pops into your mind, write it down. Keep a "Notes on the Run" book, and write down your ideas immediately after they come into your mind. Keep it by the side of your bed at night, on your desk, in your car. When you write ideas down, you can help organize and categorize them. For example, you may have a page for new sales ideas, and another for better presentations. You may have a page for closing techniques. Then you can review thoughts according to category whenever you want.

Ideas are like dreams. They tend to fade away as the day's distractions intensify. Write them down, and they are yours forever.

Stimulating Brainstorms

By sitting down, taking out a note pad, and starting to think while jotting down key words and phrases ("closing the sale," "prospecting," "time management"), you can actually stimulate brainstorms.

I know a writer who uses a similar technique to overcome her writer's block. She sits down at a word processor. If she doesn't get anywhere in a few minutes, she begins typing anyway. She types things like, "This is the first sentence of this article," or, "Come on, brain, kick in for me, will ya?" Soon, she says, the ideas start flowing.

My ideas come because I collect them in a handwritten idea book with several sections. Some of them are quite detailed, others are hurriedly jotted down. They are not all very clear, but they do remind me of things that I want to work on.

I write ideas down as they come up. I might have one page for a certain project I have in mind. I might keep that page all year long. The page might be reserved for an idea that I'm trying to develop and potential attendees of a meeting that I want to hold.

I could never sit down some morning and come up with all of the names. I wouldn't think of all of them. I collect names and ideas for meetings a year in advance sometimes. The names and the other ideas are the heart of a plan. By writing it down ahead of time, *the work is half finished before I even begin implementing the plan.*

So I write things down as I think of them. It helps me to brainstorm and to plan for projects in advance.

••

Trade Secret #53

Capture Your Brainstorms

Get a small note pad (examples shown below) or $3'' \times 5''$ note cards, and get into the habit of locking up your brainstorms. They are valuable endowments from your subconscious. Don't waste them.

NOTES ON THE RUN·

THINGS-TO-DO

REMINDER
Who should I see, call, write or thank today?

Trade Secret #54

Proving the Value of Life Insurance

- If you don't die before age 65, you will die after age 65. No one has a lease on life. It's bad enough to die. . . . Don't do it for free.
- With term insurance, you have to die in order to win. According to studies, less than 1 percent of term policies result in a death claim being paid because they are either dropped or converted to permanent insurance. In other words, you have to get lucky with term insurance in order to win. Most people would not consider dying to be lucky.
- With permanent insurance you are not spending money, you are saving it. You are merely moving money from one bank to another type of bank—one that gives you a better rate of return over the long haul and that is self-completing in the event of death or disability.
- There is no substitute for life insurance—not stocks, not bonds, not real estate, not mutual funds, not savings accounts. There is no substitute.
- Life insurance is just plain old-fashioned common sense. Nobody wants life insurance, but they do want money and what it can do for them. Life insurance is money—discounted dollars available when they are needed most.
- There is no cost to having life insurance—only a cost for not having it.
- Let's put the premium and the problem in perspective. The premium is not the problem. The premium is the solution. The problem is the problem.

30 *The Psychological Edge*

Having once decided to achieve a certain task, achieve it at all costs of tedium and distaste. The gain in self-confidence of having accomplished a tiresome labor is immense.

—ARNOLD BENNETT

A friend of mine, Larry Wilson, formerly of the Wilson Learning Corporation, says that there are four different types of personalities: analytical, expressive, driver, and amiable. Each of the personality types possesses unique qualities. Recognizing these qualities in prospects can help you make sales.

•••

Trade Secret #55

Traits of the Four Major Personality Types

The Driver
  likes to be in charge
  is very direct
  wants information quickly and to the point

The Analytical
  wants a lot of information
  is typically very neat
  is precise, concerned with detail
  is very logical

The Amiable
  responds emotionally
  wants to be well-liked
  buys from the heart if responsive to you
  is receptive if the product will help him or her fit in or belong

The Expressive
  responds emotionally
  is especially interested in self-expression
  wants to make his or her own choices

Adapt your sales style to appeal to each of these four personality types, and you will see immediate improvement in your sales income. Also, once you've applied these principles enough, you will be amazed at the insights they provide.

••

31 *Different Folks, Different Strokes*

Two roads diverged in a wood, and I—
I took the one less traveled by,
And that has made all the difference.

—ROBERT FROST

Everybody is different, and everybody wants something different. The better you are at identifying what someone wants, the better you will be at providing it to him or her. You must be creative and use your listening skills to understand what the prospect is looking for and to provide what he or she wants.

You have to approach each prospect in the right way. But the creativity necessary keeps you always on your toes.

The "Wisdom" of Investing the Difference

- Eat ham without eggs—and invest the difference.

- Don't send your children to college—and invest the difference.

- Get rid of your kids, take in boarders—and invest the difference.

- Sell your car, buy a moped—and invest the difference.

- Sell your home, move into a dump—and invest the difference.

- Stop taking showers, walk in the rain—and invest the difference.

- Stop reading, ask your friends what's going on—and invest the difference.

- Don't buy a radio, hum—and invest the difference.

- Cease planning, ad-lib—and invest the difference.

- Don't vacation, just look at travel brochures—and invest the difference.

- Sleep less, moonlight more—and invest the difference.

- Give lip service, not real service—and invest the difference.

- Don't pay taxes, go to jail—and invest the difference.

- Cancel your permanent insurance, buy term insurance—and invest the difference.

••

Trade Secret #56

"You Say No, But Your Eyes Say Yes"

Study prospect's body language. It can give you clues as to how you're being received.

Interested prospects face you and seem alert, often nodding slightly in agreement with what you are saying.

Prospects who are *turned off* by your message often have their hands folded across their chest and are looking down.

Unsure, anxious, or *tense* prospects may doodle, look away from you for extended periods, restlessly handle objects or clothing, or fidget by touching their nose, ears, or face.

When prospects feel like they are experts on a certain subject, they often drum their fingers on the table impatiently. This is your cue to now listen carefully.

Be aware, however, that simply reading body language is not enough. Body language can help, but it can't replace knowing your product and knowing your customer. It should not be relied on as a sole source of information about your prospect.

••

Part Five

Selling Up a Storm

32 *The Sales Process*

Your life IS my business!

—*ANONYMOUS*

Selling is a process.

Successful selling can be accomplished via your own personal style, but you have to stay within a broad brush framework of proven principles. You need to manage your time, take care of yourself by exercising and eating good food, and live the way you want to be treated.

Specifically, you first need to create an endless chain of prospects and keep your system going—no matter what. You must get in the door many times. When prospecting, remember the lead dog theory: If you are not the lead dog, the view never changes. You have to be the lead dog finding new prospects. It's got to be a major effort for you.

The second step is discovery. Find out what the prospect wants and try to supply it. No one cares how much you know until they see how much you care. So spend a great deal of time discovering and building the relationship. You want to increase "task tension" and reduce "relationship tension."

Next, present a win-win solution that fulfills the prospect's needs. Try to dig one tunnel. If the prospect is digging a tunnel from one side, you must dig the same tunnel from the other side. You don't want to be digging two tunnels, or you'll never meet halfway. Making a presentation that leads to one tunnel is what presenting is all about.

You then want to answer objections, but don't copy. Be creative. Make sure your answers to objections are not the old, trite, tired junk that nobody wants to hear because they've heard it so many times before. Use objection-resolvers that are meaningful and that relate to what you have already learned during your discovery activities. This makes the client feel that you understand his or her problem because you have taken the time to find out what it is!

Next get the order. If you have correctly spent a great deal of time in the discovery and prospecting modes, the presentation is more effective and takes less time. After that, the close is assumed and your getting the order is easy.

Closing is not a separate process. It is the entire process—from the beginning to the end. You begin closing the moment you say hello until you finally get the check.

After the order you've got to do what you promised. Promise a lot and deliver more.

After you get the order and fulfill your promises, get referrals. This starts the whole process again.

You must keep the system going.

Do some prospecting.

Get in the door.

Do the discovery.

Answer objections.

Get the order.

Promise a lot, deliver more.

Get referrals.

The sales process is a constant flow. It should be an endless chain of people, information, and orders. If you do it right, you'll never run out of prospects.

••

Trade Secret #57

The Rules of Selling

Learn and use these simple rules of selling, and your closing rate will jump immediately.

- Establish your credibility.
- Know the product.
- Know your client.
- Keep it simple.
- Sell concepts and benefits.
- Communicate your enthusiasm.
- Take a chance.
- Never let up!

••

33 *Prospecting*

Don't let today's solution turn into tomorrow's problem.

—ANONYMOUS

Prospect every moment of your waking life.

Always prospect. Always think about whom you can sell to next. Who needs your services? Where is there a problem you could fix?

Don't have ready-made solutions and then go looking for problems. Instead, go looking for problems needing creative solutions. You're really an idea person. You should be coming up with ideas and solutions to problems that you *uncover,* but don't have solutions in your pocket and then go looking for the problems that fit them.

Getting in the Door via Prospecting

Getting in the door is the first step.

There are several ways to get in the door. You can get in via direct mail, cold calls (or telemarketing), going door-to-door to see people, networking, and referrals. You may want to devise your own unique and interesting ways to get in the door. Find a way that works for you—just as long as it gets you in the door.

One of the things we do in our agency is to require that our agents make 100 cold phone calls a week. Each agent has to make 100 cold phone calls—*without fail.* On the average—and this is an extremely important point—this effort will produce ten appointments and, it is hoped, two sales. This applies to all agents.

Incidentally, it doesn't have to be 100 phone calls. It could be 100 pre-approach letters or direct mail solicitations.

I still make the calls each week myself, despite that fact that over the years I've created a referral network that generates lead after lead. But I'm not complacent. I have to keep going. I just never let up.

For example, if I'm riding on an airplane I may meet someone. I'll get his or her card, and later I'll call. If I see somebody's name in the newspaper, I'll pick up a phone and say, "I saw the great write-up about you, and I want to talk to you about it."

A lot of people are not interested. But I don't care about them, because a lot of other people *are* interested.

There are many other ways to do it, but going the route of 100 phone calls each week teaches you some fabulous things about discipline, consistency, rejection, and, thankfully, payoffs. If you use this method, you should call 100 people in a specific geographic area who all share common socioeconomic characteristics. This doesn't mean you must stick with that group, but it is more efficient to work one type of group at a time. The prospects might all be business owners who have the same number of employees, small businesses, or people with incomes of $100,000 or more.

Your calls must be carefully planned. Make a list of names before placing any calls. Remember, the calls count whether you make them or a telemarketer makes them. But insist on at least 100 phone calls. The system will not work without discipline.

You might make 100 calls on Monday, or 20 each day of the week, or 50 in each of two days. It doesn't matter. *As long as you make them.* If you make more calls, the system will succeed to an even greater degree.

If you also get referrals, you might cut the 100 phone calls each week down to maybe 20 phone calls. You won't have to call as many people because you'll have a better inside track. You'll be working smarter. And when you add working harder to the formula, stand back.

If you work referrals by sending letters in advance, you probably will do even better. It's also often helpful to ask a prospect who makes a referral to call the referral for you. That way, they'll expect you, and you'll need even fewer calls to make ten appointments.

You'll learn to work smarter getting in the door. In life insurance sales, it is both quality and quantity that add up to success. If you really want to stand out in the crowd and help somebody, call the people you think everybody else is calling.

What?

That's right! Call the people *you think* everybody else is calling.

Do you know why?

It is a figment of the agent's imagination to think that the prospect you want to sell to the most has been called a thousand times. Usually he or she hasn't been called at all, or if so, nowhere nearly as often as you would believe. Try it and prove it to yourself. I'll bet that the richest person in the world has not been called even once.

You know the old story: Everybody thinks that the prettiest woman in town is busy on Saturday night. Yet, she stays home alone watching television because everybody thinks she's already busy. They don't call her, so she just sits there.

Make the call!

The same thing happens with the richest prospect. Everybody's calling "Joe Lunchbucket" who has no money and no need. Everybody's banging on doors, and if they do get in, the people inside haven't got much money to spend anyway.

You want to go where there's some affluence and make the calls. You'll probably be surprised to find that you're the only one calling. And if you do run into somebody who's already bought or has an agent, say thank you very much. Next case.

That's really all you can do. Keep on going. That's the process, just keep on going.

If you make 100 calls, we know in advance that on average 90 people are going to say no and ten will say yes. Because you don't know which 90 will say no, you've got to call the whole group of 100. If the first ten calls became appointments, you could throw the next 90 away, but then it never happens that way. It's almost always the last few calls that are buyers.

It doesn't seem fair, but that's the process. You must make the calls.

One hundred calls a week is about 5,000 calls a year. Ten appointments a week is 500 appointments a year. If you make one or two sales each week, that's 50 or 100 sales a year.

If it bothers you that you have to make 5,000 calls to make 100 sales, you're not getting the big picture. Look at it this way: If each sale is worth $1,500 to $2,000, you've earned $150,000 to $200,000 each year.

Are you doing better than that now?

••

Trade Secret #58

Seven Keys to Successful Prospecting

1. Realize that selling is a numbers game. Get more *no*'s and you'll get more *yes*'s.
2. Recognize that people *want* to see you and will be receptive when you use the right approach.
3. Learn how to use the phone effectively.
4. Get referrals.
5. Use your creativity to get in the door.
6. Be ready to take advantage of any opportunity to sell.
7. Follow up with past customers and contacts for extra sales.

••

34 *Discovery*

I think I know what you mean, but I am not sure that what I heard is what you meant to say.

—ANONYMOUS

The next step after you get in the door is called the process of *discovery*. What you discover falls into two basic categories: First, you discover what your prospect's need is; and second, you discover what to do to eventually close the deal.

You should probably take notes during the discovery process so that you remember all that is said during the meeting. Be sure to ask permission to take notes because people like to know when you're gathering data on them. It shows that you respect them and consider the information important enough to record.

Occasionally, some people will say, "I don't want you taking notes," or, "I don't want to give you all that information."

You can often overcome this objection by simply asking permission. Asking permission from a prospect makes him or her a participant in solving the problem. It shows that you're working with the prospect in the way that he or she feels most comfortable. You want to emphasize the fact that what you're doing it for is his or her benefit.

You might want to explain the discovery process to the prospect. For example, you might say to the prospect, "I'll tell you why I asked to take notes. I'm going to ask you a lot of questions and get all the information from you that I need in my discovery process. Then, I hope, I'll be able to give you a lot of specific answers. When I finish reviewing all the information you give me, I'm going to send you a letter, the very next morning, outlining all the things I think I heard you say. I want you to look the information over. I want you to listen to the problems I detected. Then I'm going to ask you to respond so that I know I'm on the right track.

"I take notes for my benefit, so I can do my homework. I don't want to be working to help you solve one problem, when you're thinking about another problem. By asking you to review my report, I will know that I understand exactly what you want me to do for my homework assignment.

"When I come back here to do my presentation, I hope that my assignment will give me the answers to the questions you raised in discovery."

The discovery process is important in identifying and understanding the prospect's problem. You might understand the bulk of the problem, but there may also be something peripheral that you can do to help a prospective client.

For example, you may hear something during your conversation that has nothing to do with what you sell. It may be a personal problem that you can help with. Even though it has nothing to do with insurance sales, put it in your notes. You might offer to help with the personal problem so that the prospect knows you care. Then your presentation becomes a real cinch.

Show that you care each time.

Every gesture you make adds value to how a prospect feels about the situation. If you can start adding value during discovery process, rather than at the service end, you're way ahead of the game.

This is what makes discovery very important.

••

Trade Secret #59

Sixteen Ways To Turn Adding Value into Sales

1. Use a service call to get more sales or referrals.
2. Follow up and offer your services again.
3. Stay in touch with your customers.
4. Know the benefits of your product or service down cold.
5. Know the major reasons why people buy your product or service.
6. Suggest ways for people to pay for what they want or need.
7. Think of additional benefits.
8. Find out all that you can about your customer, so that you can target problems with a rifle, not a shotgun.
9. Customize your product or service.
10. Become an information gatherer and get feedback on what people want—then provide it.
11. Be open to changing the products or services you offer.
12. Keep up with what's happening in your industry.

13. Stress *value* to customer, not costs.
14. Show the customer how to save money or protect or increase an investment.
15. Add spice to make your product or service look good.
16. Use visual aids to emphasize benefits and value.

••

Trade Secret #60

The Job Recruiting Technique

Describe the following scenario to a prospect: You are trying to recruit an executive who is currently talking with your competition. The salary offers from all firms are about the same, as are the stock options and other fringe benefits. How are you going to get the executive to join your company?

"If you offered the job candidate $1.5 million, do you think he or she would be interested?" you might ask.

Make a recommendation: Why not offer the executive $1.5 million to join your company? That's right, $1.5 million! The company agrees to pay the executive $100,000 per year for 15 years upon retirement. If the executive dies prior to retirement, the company agrees to pay his or her family $100,000 per year for ten years.

Clarify the cost: What will it cost your company if you don't hire the executive?

Assuming the executive is about age 40, this executive compensation plan will cost your company about $10,000 per year for seven years only, and, ultimately, the company will recapture all of its cost. So think about it. Your company will recover all of its investment.

••

35 *Presentations*

Remember, nobody cares how much you know, until they know how much you care.

—*ANONYMOUS*

To close faster, more often, and for larger amounts, you need to develop a "win-win" presentation, which means that you and the prospect dig one tunnel. You must see to it that the prospect gets exactly what he or she wants or asked for in discovery. You must meet the prospect and offer a solution to his or her problems.

You can only deliver what a prospect wants if you have listened carefully. You can listen a prospect into a sale much better than you can talk him into a sale. That is, if you understand the problem, do your homework properly, and make sure your presentation relates to what you heard, you should hit right on target every time.

The prospect wins and you win.

You win by making a sale; the prospect wins by getting what he or she wants.

To me, meeting in one tunnel and developing a win-win relationship is very important.

••

Trade Secret #61

Reasons Power Words and Expressions Are So Powerful

Power words and expressions have a direct impact on the money you earn in life insurance sales. Words and expressions convey not only information to prospects, but many other confidence-instilling feelings.

Power words and expressions can

- Appeal to the person's sense of pride
- Give the person recognition for achievement
- Express appreciation and understanding
- Reach out to people for support
- Provide reassurance
- Help to make a connection with others

- Emphasize benefits
- Offer material or personal gain

··

Trade Secret #62

Power Expressions

Power expressions emphasize benefits and promote emotional appeal, just like power words.

Some examples are as follows:

- That's a great idea!
- I understand.
- Thank you.
- Will you help me?
- Will you do me a favor?
- You can trust me.

What are some phrases and expressions that are powerful for you? Write them down. You may want to ask others what expressions are powerful and appealing to them and add theirs to your list.

_____

_____

_____

_____

_____

_____

_____

··

Trade Secret #63

Power Words

Power words can make you money! They emphasize benefits and promote emotional appeal.

Some examples are as follows:

Results
Discover
Proven
Guaranteed
Easy
New
Improved
Safe
Money
Please

What are some words that are powerful for you? Write down any you think of or ask others what words are powerful and appealing to them.

_____

_____

_____

_____

_____

_____

_____

•••

36 *The Six-Step Presentation*

Sow a thought, and you reap an act;
Sow an act, and you reap a habit;
Sow a habit, and you reap a character;
Sow a character, and you reap a destiny.

—*ANONYMOUS*

My presentation binder has six tabs that show each of the following six steps:

1. Facts
2. Problems
3. Solutions
4. Recommendations
5. Action Plans
6. Miscellaneous

The facts are nothing more than what the prospective client tells me, only they are typed and reformatted. I want to be sure we're digging one tunnel toward each other so that it will meet precisely in the middle. So in the same section I usually have a letter to the client restating the facts that I gathered. Before going any further, I ask if the information is correct and whether I have heard correctly. I nail that down to make sure that we both understand what we're talking about.

At the second tab in the binder, "Problems," I point out the problems that jumped off the page for me. These are the ones that I think are urgent and must be addressed. "Let me share them with you and see if they're right," I might say. "Do you agree that paying of your estate tax is important, that the eventuality of your retirement at age 58 is an important issue for you? How about the care of your children, and their college education?"

After I get the problems down correctly, I make some recommendations. I go to the "solutions" tab in my binder. I go over four or five possible solutions that I think will solve the problems.

Then I make one recommendation that I think will fix the problems. I lay it out.

Finally, I go into the "Action Plan" section of the binder. If the client agrees with my recommendation, I detail the action plan. We discuss medical exams, applications, payment, documentation, and legal aspects. I take care to lay out all the miscellaneous things that must be done. In short, I've covered all the bases.

I've restated the facts—that's my discovery.

I've offered some problems that I think need attention.

I've looked at some solutions to solve those problems.

I've made *one* specific recommendation, not a choice of two. If I give two choices, the prospect has to go home and think about it. If I give one choice, the prospect will usually take it.

I don't want to put any obstacles in the way by forcing the prospect to decide. It's my job to figure out the best alternative.

I'm in the business to decide.

••

Trade Secret #64

Mannequins Don't Buy Policies

Decision makers can sign policy applications, but very few others in the organization can. Make sure the person you are speaking to is the decision maker! If you are not speaking with the decision maker, then it is impossible to get a yes answer, and you are in the business of getting yes answers. Also, you are in jeopardy of getting a door-slamming no from someone who never could have said yes. Don't get in that position.

Find out who the decision maker is, and find a way to talk to him or her.

••

Trade Secret #65

One at a Time, One at a Time!

During the course of an interview, many salespeople ask a second (or third, or fourth) question while the prospect is still responding to the first question. Ask only one question at a time.

The replies will be more comprehensive, and you will have a better understanding of what the prospect is thinking, feeling, and wondering.

••

37 *Objections*

Ah, but a man's reach should exceed his grasp,
Or what's a heaven for?

—*ROBERT BROWNING*

If you're making a presentation, you'll have objections. Otherwise you're making a speech.

You have to answer those objections in a creative and unique way so that the prospect understands the answers. Talk the prospect's language, not your language. Don't talk policy terms. Don't talk insurance jargon. Talk lay terms. When you answer objections, don't do it in old, trite ways.

Most importantly, you must learn answers to objections before you go in. They're mostly predictable.

Objections usually are some form of the following:

- No time
- No money
- No need
- No rush

You have to answer at least one of those, like, "I have no money, I can't afford it," or, "I have no need, my kids are grown."

You have to have the answers at your fingertips. They should be learned in advance, but not trite. When possible, answer questions in a way that directly relates to the prospect's situation.

••

Trade Secret #66

How To Deal with Objections Effectively

The four "Golden Rules of Objection Resolution" are

1. *Listen* to the prospect.
2. *Repeat* the objections to show you understand them.
3. *Demonstrate* why an objection isn't valid.
4. *Thank* the person for the objection. This will encourage more objections, which will lead you nearer to the close.

101

Trade Secret #67

Great Oaks Grow New Leaves Every Year

If a prospect detects and objects to your inexperience, you have a fantastic opportunity to tout the collective experience, stability, and expertise of your company team. Be prepared with information about how big, old, and respected your company is, Although your firm's A. M. Best rating is important, it may not have as dramatic an impact on a prospect as pointing out how many lives are insured by your firm or how long it's been in business.

Trade Secret #68

"Once Upon a Time"

Case histories often help inexperienced prospects get a feel for insurance products and the types of people who purchase them. Using names (they don't have to be names of actual people as long as you tell the prospect that the case histories are just examples), locations, and occupations bring the example alive. Case histories are best when kept simple and summarized on a single page.

38   *Getting the Order*

The secret of business is to know something that nobody else knows.

—ARISTOTLE ONASSIS

Getting the order—a signed application and a check—is not really a separate step if you've done your job right.

If you've gotten in the door, asked the right questions, listened to the answers, made the prospect feel comfortable, let the prospect know that you care, given the right presentation, and answered any objections properly, the order will follow naturally.

At this point in the process, the prospect should be thinking, "I guess you're right—this *is* my problem. I've defined it. I've told you what I need, and you've told me what I have to do to offset that need. I have to do something about the problem today, and I don't know any other way to do it but the way that you have showed me. I might as well give you a check."

That's the way an order should go: no misrepresentation by the salesperson and no fighting back by the prospect.

It's not I win, you lose.

It's I win, you win.

We do it together.

••

Trade Secret #69

Push for an Immediate Decision

If the prospect is wavering on a decision, you need to make it seem urgent that the prospect act immediately to get certain benefits.

Some possibilities (if applicable) are listed below.

- You have to pay now if you want the policy. I can't leave anything behind.
- If you act now, you'll get a money back guarantee.
- If you act now, you'll get an extra discount (or a bonus gift, a coupon, and so on).

- It costs less now. The price is going up soon.
- You'll find it's more convenient to buy now.
- You'll have the benefits of the product starting now.
- We're offering a special package of products or services to those who act now.

39 *Closing In on Closing*

Whatsoever thy hand findeth to do, do it with thy might.
—*ECCLESIASTES 9:10*

You must have good closing techniques.

On average, it takes five attempts to close—to convert a prospect into a client. Most salespeople don't know more than one closing technique. How can you close more than one in five times when you only know one closing technique? You have to learn at least five techniques. And you have to know them well enough—almost by instinct—to put them to use as they are required.

Closing techniques are aids that you use to help the client make a valid buying decision. They help you develop a win/win relationship, not a win/lose relationship.

You want to be able to offer the prospect what he or she wants so that you make a sale. Then when you leave, you hope the new client says, "Thank you. You really helped me. I really appreciate it."

Very few things compare to the feeling of making a wonderful sale, putting some cash in your pocket, proving that your selling system works, *and* hearing the client thank *you!* But it happens all the time when you do good discovery, when you understand the client's needs, and when you present alternative solutions to the client. The client often looks at those solutions and says, "You know what? Based on your recommendations, I think I will do this because that will give me what I want. I really appreciate this."

••

Trade Secret #70

Nutshell Review of the Major Steps to a Successful Close

1. Encourage objections and deal with them effectively.
2. Learn to wait quietly for a response after you have made a closing question. Let the prospect give you answers.
3. Turn tough questions back on your prospect by asking other questions.

4. Push for an immediate decision.
5. Let the prospect know why it is urgent to act immediately.
6. Leave the door open to follow up if you can't close immediately. Don't leave anything (besides a brochure) and say you'll call again. Leave some material (not too much) so that the person will want to seek you for more. A detailed sales brochure restates the main benefits you offer, provides reassurance about you and the company, and gives the person time to think over the main points of your offer.
7. Show the prospect how to pay for what he or she wants now. Suggest financing possibilities. Break down the total costs into smaller amounts.
8. Use an approach that suits your own style. Be creative when you close.

40 *Referrals*

In life, as in a football game, the principle to follow is: Hit the line hard.

—THEODORE ROOSEVELT

Make sure you deliver on your promises because once you do the next step becomes obvious—and wildly lucrative! It is called *referrals.*

You often won't have to ask clients to make referrals. They might say, "You know what? This is fabulous. I've got to tell my brother-in-law about this. I've got to tell my cousin about this. He's got to call you."

But you can't rely on the client to call for you. A client's offer may be sincere, but he or she will often forget to call.

No problem.

Say, "Thank you! That is a good idea. May I have your brother-in-law's name so in case you forget, I can remind you to call him for me?"

Get the referrals. If you did your job right, clients will give them to you without your asking.

For example, a 27-year-old man named Kevin came to my office and spent $20,000 for retirement income. He wasn't in my office 20 minutes. He had been a referral. "I want you to show this to my uncle," he said as he walked out the door. "It's fabulous."

He gave me his uncle's name: Phillip. "Just in case you forget," in a couple of weeks when I see you again, I'll remind you about Phillip," I said. "Is that okay with you?"

"Great, you make sure you remind me," he said.

Exactly eight days later, I had a check from Phillip for a larger policy than I sold to Kevin. Phillip then gave me the name of his business partner.

The process starts over again, and keeps repeating itself. With referrals, I get the next prospect's name and get in the door again, without making any phone calls. You don't *have* to make cold phone calls ever again if you do the process right. A good referral system can get you rich very quickly.

You should try to get two or three names from each client. If you only get one name, you're still in business. But if that one person doesn't want to see you, then you're out of the referral process and making calls again. You need to get as many names as possible so the process keeps revolving all the time.

The referral process has revolved in the very same way for me for forty years.

••

Trade Secret #71

Role Playing

Ask a prospect to role play with you. Tell the prospect to assume that he or she died last night and that you are the executor of the will.

"It's the morning after your death, and I'm sitting at my desk in my office," you might say. "There is a set of papers on my desk and your spouse is sitting opposite me. What questions do you think your spouse will ask me? Remember the assumption that you died last night, and I'm your executor. What will your spouse want to know?"

The prospect will probably correctly guess the following:

What does the will say?
How much income do I get?
How long do I get the income?
Are there some taxes to be paid?
How much do we owe?
What happens to the business?

"Now we're not finished," you say. "The same afternoon, the manager of the business is coming in to see me. What will the manager want to know?"

Run down the business manager's likely questions.

Do I have a job?
Will the business continue?
How do we deal with the bank?
And whom do I report to?

"Earlier that day, the banker called," you continue. "The banker had some questions for me as the executor."

Go over the banker's possible questions.

Who's going to run the business?
How will the bank loan get repaid?
Was there any life insurance?

•••

Part Six

Never Let Up!

41 *The Myth of Only Working Smarter and Not Harder*

In the modern world of business, it is useless to be a creative original unless you can also sell what you create. Management cannot be expected to recognize a good idea unless it is presented to them by a good salesman.

—David Ogilvy

The idea that you can work smarter, but not harder, is a myth, pure and simple.

You've got to work smarter *and* harder. All the time. There is no such thing as only working smarter. That's good material for storybooks. But it doesn't work in real life.

You need to do it smarter and harder. You must use a motor *and* a sail. They work more effectively together than by themselves.

There is no way around working smarter and harder. I work 70 hours a week. That's the harder. I am also always thinking, planning, organizing, making contacts, and making calls. I never let up. That's the smarter.

If you find that you are losing now, be patient. By working both *harder* and *smarter,* you can't lose.

••

Trade Secret #72

Just Close

Close. That's right, *just close. Ask for the business.*

If you are not sure when to close, do it sooner rather than later. I can't tell you how many people fail to *ask for the business.* As a result, they don't get it.

An old story of a chief rabbi in an ancient province in Turkey applies here. The house of worship there was very small, old, and in need of many repairs and furnishings. Each morning, after the religious services, the worshipers would file out of the chapel, passing the wooden bucket the rabbi used to collect donations. The rabbi's congregation was wealthy, but only about a quarter of the worshipers made small contributions each day.

The rabbi, dismayed over the lack of funds to make necessary repairs, consulted with a merchant who was a member of the congregation. The merchant gave the rabbi an idea. The next morning, the rabbi stood at the back of the chapel after the services, held the bucket, and simply said, "Any contributions will be welcomed," as each person filed past.

That morning, and for each day thereafter, more than two thirds of the worshipers dropped money in the bucket!

Ask, and you shall receive!

42 *Zeno's Paradox*

Bite off more than you can chew,
Then chew it.
Plan more than you can do,
Then do it.

—Anonymous

Suppose you want to go from point *A* to point *B*. Because that goal seems unattainable all at once, you decide to aim for the midpoint between *A* and *B*. When you reach that goal, you are happy and decide to go halfway from the midpoint to point *B*. Once you reach the new midpoint you are happy and decide to keep going to successive midpoints. There's only one problem: Though you are always moving toward your goal, you will never reach point *B*.

Zeno, a Greek philosopher who lived around 460 B.C., first noted that paradox. It applies to the selling of life insurance as well.

In life insurance sales, between the first call and a signed application, there are an infinite number of midpoints, each with its own obstacles: objections, broken appointments, lack of funds, indecision, cheaper deals, and so on.

But the journey of a mile begins with but one step. You have to take those steps every inch of the way. But you must not confuse a midpoint for your destination. They are only milestones on your way to your goal. Never settle for halfway.

••

Trade Secret #73

Handling Questions

Four simple rules can dramatically improve the effectiveness of the way you handle questions.

1. Listen to the question.
2. Repeat it.
3. Answer it.
4. Thank the prospect.

••

43 *It Can Pay To Be Different*

Fall seven times, stand up eight!

—*JAPANESE PROVERB*

Be different just to be different. It's that simple.

Your business cards, stationery, and graphics should be unique. The way you conduct your life, the way you dress, and the way you make a presentation should all be different.

Everything should be unique so you can finish first and with the biggest prize.

Being unique is an important key to success.

Different for Difference's Sake

It pays to be different.

Find out what the world is doing, and then don't do it. That's really what it's about. When you find out what everybody else is doing, do something different.

Why?

Any given group has a few leaders and many followers. Leaders think differently than followers. They challenge custom where followers accept it. So find your niche and put your own special twist on it.

You can show you're different in many ways. Take my business card, for example. It's about one inch by one-half inch. On the front it has my name and address. On the back it reads, in type so small it is almost illegible: The size of this card is made necessary by the amount of business you've given me lately.

Unique. Different. Nobody else has that.

---

(215) 875-8700
(609) 966-5013 (MOBILE)
(800) 523-9935 (TOLL FREE)

Sidney A. Friedman, CLU
PRESIDENT

CORPORATE FINANCIAL SERVICES INC

THE SIZE OF THIS CARD
IS MADE NECESSARY BY
THE AMOUNT OF BUSINESS
YOU'VE GIVEN ME LATELY

I also have a card that looks like a page out of the yellow pages. I don't give this card to everyone. I give it to corporate presidents and other big clients, not the rank and file. It has every phone number where I can be reached: home, car, fax, office, summer home, and private lines. The yellow pages business card says to clients that if they need me, they got me.

I don't give the yellow pages card to the rank and file employees of the companies we insure because I don't want them reaching me before the president of the company can reach me.

It's not that I don't want to serve the rank and file. It's just that they don't usually decide to buy policies like the decision makers of the company do.

The car I drive is also unique: It's a Rolls convertible. Not many people have them. They only make two each week for the entire world.

I have one of them.

My house and family are also unusual.

The way I dress is unusual because I don't want to imitate anybody. I'd rather be copied. Some people may see that as being crass. I view it as being unique.

The Broadway Restaurant downstairs has a menu with sandwiches named after people. One of the sandwiches is named after me.

A friend once said, "Hey, Sid, you're the cheapest sandwich on the menu."

"Yes," I responded, "but I'm ON the menu."

In a small way, being on the menu is important. I was lucky. I met some of the management, and they put me on the menu.

Now, why is that important?

I don't know, it's part of the Sidney Friedman ambiance. The restaurant managers considered me unique enough to be put me on their menu.

Find your own ambiance and create your own style. Develop a fingerprint or a footprint of who you are.

Leave a trail that makes you proud, not embarrassed.

A good trail says, "I've been here and people are definitely better off (including me) because I was here."

That's important.

That's about being unique.

••

Trade Secret #74

Odd Man In

Make of list of the ways you can be a different life insurance professional, and find a way to proceed with at least one of them tomorrow morning. Whatever you choose, begin to develop your trademark immediately.

••

Trade Secret #75

Distinguishing Characteristics

Distinguish your product by stressing the superior service advantage your company has over others: you, your personal interest, and your commitment to the insurance business.

••

44 *Tips Open Closed Doors*

All that is necessary to break the spell of inertia and frustration, is this: Act as if it were impossible to fail. That is the talisman, the formula, the command of right-about-face which turns us from failure towards success.
—DOROTHEA BRANDE

Without getting in to see people, your chances of succeeding in life insurance sales dry up.

To get the doors open, I like to offer prospects helpful tips that they appreciate.

I might ask, "Are you paying for your insurance with before-tax dollars or, like most people, with after-tax dollars? In other words, are you paying for it from your personal checkbook, or are you using your corporate checkbook to buy your insurance? Most people use their personal checkbook. Can I show you how to use your corporate checkbook?"

Or I might ask, "Do your policies work the old way or the new way?"

"New way?" the prospect than asks. "What's the new way?"

Get the prospect thinking about new ways to conduct business or life. You might ask, "May I show you a way to keep key people in your business?" or, "May I help to insure one year's profits?"

Offering helpful tips can make getting in the door easier.

Light the Fuse on Your Way Out

I always try to leave clients with thoughts or information that trigger their memory later so that they remember me when I call back.

For example, I've created a brochure about my agency. It describes who we are and what we do. I may leave it with a prospect, and when I call back, the brochure serves as a starting point for the conversation. I get the prospect to think about an issue and come back to me later.

A client of mine, a 60-year-old lawyer, told me he wanted to retire in ten years.

"Well, where will the money come from?" I asked.

"I've got three partners but there's no way they're going to have the money to buy me out ten years from now."

"You know, there's an interesting story about businesses being sold. Most people who sell their businesses fund the sale for their company with their own money. They get bought with their own money."

"What do you mean by that?"

"Well, no matter how you cut it, in a small, closely held corporation—rather than a publicly held company—if you want out, you wind up getting paid with your own money when you leave. Whether you get it over a period of years or in one lump sum makes no difference. You're getting a check that is your own money. If you don't sell it, you get the money—over a period of years—that the person who was buying it was going to get.

"But you can have your three partners buy you out instead. Here's how you do it: Raise their salary enough so that they can get the money to buy you out plus pay the tax on the money and get a tax deduction for you. You'll accomplish everything at one time."

He ended up doing just that. His three partners bought him out with the money he gave them to buy him out over the ten years.

The point is to *suggest something creative!* Be creative in your ideas. Trigger thoughts that will help the client understand a problem better. It's all part of discovery. You should spend a lot of time finding out what the client wants and then provide it.

So even though you're helping yourself with the dream, you're helping your client with his or her dream. Help the client dream better.

•••

Trade Secret #76

"Never Ever" Is a Long Time

I don't know how many of you have children who use the expression "never ever," but mine did. For example, "Never ever touch the stove when it's on. . . . it is hot and will burn you." Thus, the term in our family stated universal truths.

At a recent meeting, an agent made a statement that was almost impossible to believe. "If you put away $2,000 each year for ten years at 7 percent interest, and then let it ride at 7 percent forever, you'll have more money than if you started in the eleventh year and put away $2,000 at 7 percent every year to age 65. Regardless at what age you start, you'll never, ever catch it!"

A Doubting Thomas present said, "That is impossible!"

So, using my calculator, I started at age 6 hypothetically and here are the results:

Age 6–15: $2,000 per year @7% for 10 years: $ 31,567
Age 16–65: $31,567 @7% to age 65 (50 years): $929,876
Age 16–65: $2,000 per year @7% for 50 years: $871,972

"That's unbelievable!" said Doubting Tom. "I wonder what happens in a whole life contract if I do that?"

I used age 1 and age 11 and got the *same result!*

Conclusion

1. Show this to Grandpa and Grandma and see if they'd like to start a program today for their grandchildren.
2. Put that $2,000 IRA money into a whole life policy.
3. Return on a whole life policy is about 7% . . . Not Bad.
4. "Never ever" is a long time.

[Thanks to James A. Urner for this one.]

•••

Trade Secret #77

Sample Letter To Present Retirement Planning

[Date]

Mr. Bobby Bigg
345 Cinclair Road
Downtown, PA 23491

Dear Mr. Bigg:

If you would kindly provide us with your date of birth below, we will be happy to send you information on a retirement/savings plan that will offer you with the following benefits:

- A retirement plan that will grow on *a tax-deferred basis.*
- A retirement income to you even if you decide to retire *before age 59½ without penalty.*
- Automatic contributions on your behalf if you are *disabled.*
- A retirement income to your *spouse* if you die *prematurely.*
- Permission to contribute *an unlimited amount* to this program.
- *Tax-free income* received by you or your spouse.

This is one of the most talked about retirement plans available in the United States today!

Sincerely,

Al Agent

....

45 Listening for a Sale

If you are speaking and not getting a reaction, well, you are just making a speech.

—*Anonymous*

Many great salespeople have said that no one has ever listened himself or herself out of a job.

It is a fact that you can sell more by listening than you can by talking. You can actually listen the prospect into a sale. Let the prospect speak. Find out something about the prospect. Discovery is the most important piece of the puzzle.

You might have heard the theory of the two triangles.

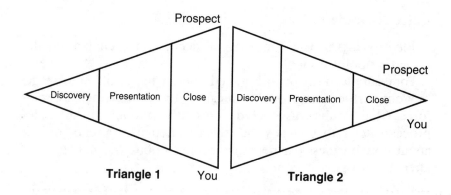

Let's say you begin the process in the smaller end of triangle 1, where you do discovery. You spend only a little time on discovery and then move to the larger section of the triangle, where you do presentation. Finally, in the largest end you do close, on which you spend the most time.

But you'll notice that you and the prospect are at opposite ends of the triangle. You didn't spend enough time in discovery— finding the facts—therefore, what you're presenting is not addressing the client's need.

You should do it the other way around, like in triangle 2, and spend a great deal of time in discovery so your presentation is easier. By the time you finally get to the close, you and the prospect have moved together. The close is a given.

Your prospect will say, "You know what, you understand my problem. You're presenting it the way I understand it; therefore, let's do it."

Otherwise you may come off sounding like a salesman who thinks, "I'm not quite sure what you need. I'm going to make a presentation that's good for me—although it may not be so good for you."

That won't get you anywhere.

••

Trade Secret #78

Drive It Home

Identify a prospect's motive, or need, and then continually drive that point home.

For example, if the prospect needs money to pay off a mortgage, buy out partners, or provide education and other expenses, reinforce what you've discovered constantly throughout the sales process. Refer to colleges that the children may attend, or ask about how business partners may behave in buy-out negotiations after the prospect is gone.

••

46   *Let the Phone Ring*

If you have built castles in the air, your work need not be lost. That is where they ought to be. Now, build foundations under them.

—HENRY DAVID THOREAU

Who calls someone on the telephone and hangs up after one ring? Yet, by not following up, that is exactly what you are doing. If it's worth doing one time, it's worth following up.

If you're going to send a letter to offer someone the opportunity to buy life insurance, then you should follow up with a phone call. If all you're going to do is send a letter and wait for a reply, you're wasting your time. You'll get a 0.5 percent response rate. The other 99.5 percent who didn't respond also buy insurance. So if you're going to write them a letter, call them and talk about the letter you sent to them. Follow up.

If you write it in your plan to do it, make sure you actually get it done. It takes discipline to make sure it gets done.

••

Trade Secret #79

Smile When You Say That

Make a point of smiling when you pick up the telephone.

A smile can actually be heard! If you are skeptical of this, try this experiment: Call a local friend and say that you are going to call back three times. State that during one of the calls, you will be smiling. Ask your friend to guess which one.

According to Telephone Communications Consultants, Inc., the correct answer is identified 78 percent of the time.

••

Trade Secret #80

"Gee, What a Coincidence"

If you are having a difficult time getting through to a prospect on the telephone, try calling a little after noon, when regular secretaries are often out to lunch. The boss may answer his or her own phone, or, the fill-in secretary may be less likely to turn you away.

Or, call early in the morning (before nine o'clock) or late in the day (after five o'clock) when much of the support staff is not around and top executives are most likely to answer their own phones.

••

47 *Easing into a Good Sales Presentation*

If you aren't fired with enthusiasm, you will be fired with enthusiasm.

— VINCE LOMBARDI

There are two kinds of tension, task tension and relationship tension. When you meet somebody for the first time, the relationship tension is high.

Will I say the right thing?

Will I get tongue-tied?

Do I look good?

Will I appear like the professional I want to be?

The first thing you want to do is reduce the relationship tension by being low key until you get something going. Use eye contact, dress properly, and plan a presentation. Don't try to wing it— understand what you're going to say before you say it. Don't do ready, fire, aim. Instead, try ready, aim, *fire*.

Once you've reduced relationship tension, you can reveal the reason you're there. You can move into high gear and really get into the task.

"Hey, while we're talking about your estate," you might say, "Let's discuss how your $10 million estate has a $5 million tax liability and how I can get rid of it for $500,000. No matter what you, your accountant, or your attorney have done, your $10 million estate has a $5 million estate tax lien. Everybody has told you that. The only question now is, what's the cheapest way to get that $5 million? How do you do that? I can reduce it to $500,000. I can go to the IRS for you today and make a deal with them to negotiate your $5 million in taxes down to $500,000. I can get a paid bill from them right now. I will say, 'Mr. Jones has a $10 million estate. He's got a $5 million tax liability. If I give you $500,000 now, IRS, will you wipe out his tax when he and his wife die?' And if they say yes, do you want it?"

That's a presentation of what can be done through life insurance. If I can whet a prospect's appetite, I'm on my way.

Learn to take advantage of life insurance's leverage quality through the creative use of life insurance policies.

"It takes about ten cents on the dollar to buy a life insurance policy over a lifetime," I might explain continuing my presentation. "That means that if you give me $500,000 today, I will buy a one-payment life insurance policy on your life worth $5 million. If you can't afford $500,000 today, give me $50,000 a year for ten years. I'll still make the deal with the IRS. When you die, I'll go to the IRS and hand them the $5 million that I promised. It cost you only $500,000. Your debt to the IRS is canceled because you bought life insurance for $5 million.

"That's what I do for a living. I provide money cheaper than you can find it elsewhere. I discount your estate taxes by 90 cents on the dollar. Whether it's a retirement plan, life insurance plan, or key employee benefit plan, you will never give the insurance company more than ten cents on the dollar. As an investment, there's none better. You give me ten cents, I'll give you a dollar every time. Give me $500,000, and I'll give you $5 million."

That's the way to sell insurance.

....

Trade Secret #81

Balancing the Tension in Your Initial Presentation

The stages in balancing relationship tension and task tension in an initial presentation are shown below.

Stage 1:   Initial Contact Phase
            Relationship tension: high
            Task tension: low
            Your job: build rapport

Stage 2:   Transition Phase
            Relationship tension: moderately high
            Task tension: moderately low
            Your job: gradually shift conversation to the purpose of your call

Stage 3:   Presentation Phase
          Relationship tension and task tension in balance
          Your job: make your best presentation

●●●

Trade Secret #82

How Are Death Taxes Paid?

Death taxes are due and are payable in cash within nine months after a taxpayer's death. Five ways to provide money for death taxes are as follows:

1. The executor may borrow the cash.
    This only defers the problem, since the money will have to be repaid with interest. This includes installment payments to the government.
2. The taxpayer may pay in cash.
    A person rarely accumulates large sums of cash. To do so, the person probably must forgo many profitable investment opportunities in order to keep the estate liquid.
3. The taxpayer may sell stock market investments.
    This may be a wise choice if the market is up when the stocks or bonds need to be converted to cash and the taxpayer has been investing long enough to have accumulated the necessary amount.
4. The executor may liquidate other assets.
    If there is not a ready market, however, the assets may be sold at a great loss.
5. The taxpayer can pay estate settlement costs with life insurance. Some advantages of life insurance are as follows:

    a. Dollars are "discounted." The taxpayer's heirs always get back more than what was paid.
    b. Payment of benefit is prompt.
    c. There is no income or capital gain tax on the proceeds.
    d. It can be estate tax free.
    e. Payments can be spread out rather than coming all at once.

    f.   It avoids all the problems of the other four methods set forth above.

    g. Life insurance provides cash for a predictable and certain need that will arise at some unpredictable moment.

•••

48 *You Must Look Good...To You*

Vive la différence!

—FRENCH EXPRESSION

Staying physically fit is very important in maintaining a positive self-image.

You have to take care of your body and your mind. Exercise, eat well, and maintain a healthy weight. You can't keep your mind fit unless your body is fit. Look good so that you feel good.

It's obvious that if you don't like the way you look in the mirror, you're not going to feel very good about yourself. Then you won't project a good self-image. You'll lack the confidence to be a good salesperson.

When somebody says, "You wear rose-colored glasses," it means you see the positive in almost any situation. I think it's a compliment for somebody to say, "Well, you don't understand the problem. You wear rose-colored glasses."

That's right, I don't! I won't participate. I won't participate in a recession. I won't participate in downside. There is no such thing. My glasses are too rosy.

Most Important Words

The six most important words are:
   I admit I made a mistake.

The five most important words are:
   You did a good job.

The four most important words are:
   What is your opinion?

The three most important words are:
   If you please.

The two most important words are:
   Thank you.

131

The single most important word is:
   We

The single least important word is:
   I

••

Trade Secret #83

Sample Pre-Approach Letter

Fred Schwartz
ABC Corporation
123 Main Street
Anywhere, CA 94104

Dear Mr. Schwartz:

Attached to this letter is a tax-free dollar.

Within the next ten days, I will call you to arrange an appointment to show you how successful individuals are using tax-free and tax-deferred dollars to:

- Enhance their own retirement income
- Maximize their pension benefits
- Protect their families
- Discount the impact of estate taxes
- Leverage their gifts to charity
- Facilitate the continuation of their businesses
- Reward their key employees

I genuinely look forward to meeting you.

Sincerely yours,

Sidney Friedman, CLU, ChFC

P.S. Tom Jones, for whom I recently did some planning, suggested that I write you.

Note: Staple a crisp, new $1 bill to this letter.

••

Trade Secret #84

The Right Angle

Whenever you can arrange it, be sure to sit at right angles to your prospect. Psychologists suggest that sitting face-to-face creates a challenging, adversarial environment. Sitting at right angles creates a consultative environment.

••

49 *Projecting Your Image*

Eat to please yourself; dress to please others.
—BENJAMIN FRANKLIN

Projecting your image to others is how you present yourself physically. You must leave a good first impression on prospects. Your appearance and dress are like the attractive folder on a professionally produced written presentation.

Are your clothes pressed?

Are you well-groomed?

Many things make up your persona. Do you look as good as you can look?

The client expects performance from you because you look like you're going to provide it. Concentrate on projecting a confident, successful image even before meeting with clients. Approach meetings with the knowledge that there is something special and different about you. Your appearance must say to the client or prospect, "I know what I'm talking about. You can trust me."

Part of your image should include showing how much you care. The adage that people don't care how much you know till they know how much you care is very important. They don't care if you are the smartest person in the whole world. If they think you don't care, they won't trust you. So, first, teach them to trust you.

If they trust you, the rest is easy.

It Pays To Be an Expert

A prospect is calling on me for expertise.

What do I recommend?

When I go to a doctor, the doctor doesn't tell me that I have either athlete's foot or an ear infection and then let me choose which one. The doctor determines what my problem is and recommends treatment. The doctor evaluates health data and then makes a decision. If the doctor is good, he or she won't need to run a lab test to diagnose the ear infection. The doctor's seen it a million times before. He or she makes decisions based on principles similar to my 80/20/100/51 rule.

Thus, when prospects call on you for advice, give it to them. Be
authoritative, professional, knowledgeable.

That's what they expect from you. That's also why they'll buy
from you.

••

Trade Secret #85

Tea for Two

Invite your prospect to see your office.

This technique tells the prospect that you are proud of your organization and want to show it off. It also tells the prospect that
you are a force to be reckoned with—not the stereotypical door-
to-door salesperson.

If your offices are not opulent, make the invitation anyway.
People like to feel welcomed. The invitation puts you on equal
footing with prospects since they are meeting you in your surroundings.

I've found that prospects are more likely to come in if I ask
them *when* they would like to come in, rather than *whether* or not
they would.

••

Trade Secret #86

Don't Knock the Competition

Praise the competition, but praise your company even more.

Unless you are confident that your prospect is about to be defrauded in some way, never knock the competition. After all, your
competitor and you are in the same industry.

By praising the competition, you reinforce the validity and utility of insurance. At the crucial moment, however, you should state
several reasons why your company's product will most effectively
solve the prospect's problem.

••

Trade Secret #87

Raise Your Own Objections

When *you* make an objection to a possible plan before a prospect does, it shows that you are well-prepared, on your toes, and alert to the prospect's specific situation. It shows you're not out to make a quick, easy sale. Anticipate potential problems, and beat the prospect to the punch!

••

50 *Speaking of Acting*

I know you think you understand what you thought I said, but I'm not sure that what you thought you heard is what I meant to say.

—ANONYMOUS

Practice what you are going to say to prospects.

Make sure that you speak well, that you have something to say, that your ideas are in the right order. Make your ideas believable.

Can you act? It's a very important skill.

Can you be an actor? A chameleon?

Can you adjust your personality to be like your client's? Can you adopt qualities of the personality types I mentioned (the driver, analytical, amiable, and expressive) to complement the personality of your client?

That's not manipulative. It's just giving the client what he or she feels most comfortable with so he or she can feel comfortable with you. If that requires you to be a chameleon at times, that's okay. When you're doing it right, you get an understanding of the prospect's needs, and you can help find first-class solutions.

••

Trade Secret #88

Expressions To Avoid

Turning a prospect off can blow a sale and a relationship. Think before you speak, and consider eliminating the following expressions from your vocabulary.

Expressions to avoid:	Why:	Use instead:
What I'm trying to say . . .	Suggests that the person is dumb and can't understand you	In short . . . (or just summarize message)

Expressions to avoid:	Why:	Use instead:
In other words . . .	Suggests that the person hasn't understood you the first time	To summarize . . .
Let me be honest with you . . .	Suggests you've been lying all along	—
You know . . .	Is meaningless and sounds bad	—

Words to avoid:	Why:	Use instead:
Sales or sold	No one wants to be sold; they prefer to buy or own	Involved or own
Contract	Sounds too legal	Agreement, paperwork, memo of understanding
Sign	Sounds too final and formal	Endorse or okay
Pitch	Sounds too pushy and unprofessional	Presentation
Deal	Sounds too unprofessional	Opportunity

51 *Using Overhead Projectors*

Nothing is particularly hard if you divide it into small jobs.

—Henry Ford

Using an overhead projector is often helpful in sales.

Overhead projectors are simple to use, and overhead visuals are easy to make. You don't have to turn the lights out to operate overhead projectors, so you can maintain eye contact with the client.

Whether you have one person or ten people in the room, it's a wonderful way to take control and hold attention. People listen to your message like children in a schoolroom.

••

Trade Secret #89

Create Your Own Visual Aids

Check off or list below what visual aids you need for a current project. Types of visual aids you might use include props, flip charts, a blackboard, slides, or signs, overheads (and projector).

Guide to Using Visuals

Project for which visuals will be used: _____

Props needed:

To buy: _____

_____

_____

_____

To make: _____

_____

_____

_____

Flip chart:

    Easel   _____

    Pad of paper   _____

    Felt-tip markers   _____

    (colors needed: _____)

Overheads:

    Number of blanks needed   _____

    Copy   _____

    Number of prepared overheads   _____

    Artwork   _____

    Crayons/pencils for drawing   _____

    (colors needed: _____)

Overhead projector:

    Bring myself   _____   Provided   _____

Blackboard:

    Bring myself   _____   Provided   _____

    Chalk   _____   (colors needed: _____)

Slides:

    Carousel projector   _____   Copy   _____

    Slide trays   _____

    Photographs needed   _____

Signs:

    Sign boards   _____   (colors needed: _____)

    Felt-tip markers   _____

    (colors needed: _____)

••

52 *How To Avoid Comparison Shopping*

> *Seeing is believing.*
>
> —*ANONYMOUS*

Unlike the Lone Ranger, you don't have to leave a silver bullet behind as a memento.

When you leave, don't leave your presentation. Leave nothing behind so that the prospect can't go and comparison shop on you. If the prospect wants your presentation, make him or her buy it.

I very seldom get comparison shopped because I leave very little for the customer to shop with. I may leave a brochure that lists general information, but I don't give the prospect a long-range proposal or quote. If the prospect likes my ideas, he or she buys them.

When prospects shop for cars, they don't get written proposals. When they shop for houses, they don't get written proposals. Why should I have to give one?

I never do it.

When prospects buy mutual funds do they get proposals? They buy them. They say, I want two of those, three of those. It's the same thing here. If they like what you have to say and trust you—that's the issue, they trust you—they don't expect to get a proposal.

I don't leave them.

The client only gets a proposal if it's paid for.

••

Trade Secret #90

Take Your Ball Home after the Game

At the end of a meeting, slowly and carefully pick up any handouts, material, or reports that you used in your presentation and put them into your briefcase.

This has two important effects: One, it prevents prospects from shopping your quote or idea. (You don't get a proposal when you go in to buy a car or a house, do you?); and two, it creates a subtle psychological desire on the prospect's part to get back what he or she once possessed.

••

Trade Secret #91

Uncover the Real Objection

When fending off an objection based on price, keep in mind that no two proposals are identical, and therefore, a more expensive policy may actually have an even greater value than the prospect realizes.

Psychologists suggest the price-based objections are often merely screens obscuring other, solvable objections. You must probe with intelligent, informed questions to get to the source of an objection. If it really is price that is the problem, try adding more benefits and more value so that the price doesn't become the major issue.

If your quote is higher than others, explain why (better service, benefits, and so on).

Discuss the value and benefits your solution offers to the prospect's problem.

••

Trade Secret #92

Slow Responses Work Best

During a meeting with a prospect, *don't answer too quickly.*
Take a moment.

Think about how you will phrase your response, especially when you know the response well and are likely to blurt it out too quickly.

The "fast-talking salesman" may be a cliché, but pat answers tossed off matter-of-factly hurt your credibility in the prospect's eyes.

••

53

Listen to the Radio Station WII-FM

Be prepared.

What does the prospect want, and what will he or she get out of this transaction?

Why should I do it?

Every prospective client is tuned into a mental radio station: WII-FM (What's In It For Me?). They're always asking the same question. Another station that they listen to is MMFC-AM (Make Me Feel Confident About Myself). You must make them feel important.

These are AM and FM stations that prospects tune into all the time, whether you like it or not.

If I buy this, what do I get out of it?

Do I get my money's worth?

Do I get value?

They are thinking all the time. I try to put myself in their shoes.

I ask myself: If I were being offered this, what would I want to hear? And I build my presentation that way.

••

Trade Secret #93

Listen Up

Listening is more than keeping silent.

If you are merely thinking about what you're going to say next and not really listening, then you are in trouble. You are not listening, you are waiting.

There is a tremendous difference.

The best place to practice listening is when you are with people you know well, because we tend to listen less carefully to those with whom we feel comfortable.

••

54 *Self-Evaluation Is a Constant Process*

Anytime the going seems easy, you'd better check to see if you are going downhill.

—ANONYMOUS

You should constantly be evaluating where you are, where you are going, and how you will get there as you pass the checkpoints along the way.

The evaluation process is not a static thing. It's a dynamic process that changes according to where you are and what you want from it.

You develop your checkpoint and evaluation schedule *for yourself.* Not for me. Not for your spouse. Not for your district manager. For you.

Whether it's weekly, monthly, or annually, you should take time to ask, Where am I now? You should constantly be reevaluating.

I said earlier in this book that Larry Wilson is a fantastic professional. He professes three things: Be good and know it; keep on getting better; and critique your own performance. That's part of asking, Where am I now?

This constant analysis should become second nature, automatic—just like your heartbeat. It should never stop.

••

Trade Secret #94

To Err Is To Gain Respect

When you screw something up, *admit it immediately* in loud and clear terms. Nothing gains the respect of others more quickly than an open acknowledgment of a mistake.

If the prospect or client isn't too upset and tries to minimize the problem ("Well, it sounds like the actuaries erred."), that's great. But take your share of the responsibility: Perhaps they did err, but I represent Phoenix Mutual, and I am sorry about this. I'll get you a new report immediately.

••

55 *A Fear of Success*

The only thing we have to fear is fear itself.
—FRANKLIN DELANO ROOSEVELT

Most people who seem to have a strong fear of failure really have a fear of success.

On one level, they may not know how to cope with the potential implications of success. What does that mean?

Well, success is not the problem for them. It's the very real fear of doing well but *then being unable to repeat the success.*

I understand that anxiety. But it is just that—an anxiety.

To those who suffer from it, may I assure you that success has its own inertia. Sure, you may have rotten years after a great year, but once you've learned the secrets of succeeding, the lean years become exceptions.

Rich Bach, the novelist, said, "Name your limitations—and they are yours."

Trade Secret #95

Close Makes the Salesperson

Don't be afraid to close. Some people fear it because it is the moment of truth when you find out that you may have failed.

"Know the truth, and it shall set ye free."

Close early and often. You'll learn to improve your timing. Meanwhile, you'll make a lot more sales than if you hesitate, close too late, or never even try to close at all!

Trade Secret #96

How to Follow Up (If You Can't Close Now)

*   Leave some material that the person can go over, but be selective in what you leave.

- Don't leave too much. Leave the person wanting more or needing to see you again to answer additional questions.
- Include a detailed sales brochure in what you leave. A sales brochure can be beneficial because it restates the main benefits you offer, reassures the prospect of the strength and substance of your company, and gives a prospect who may feel pressured time to think over your offer.
- You may also choose to leave no information and say you'll call again later.

56 *Using the Inertia of Stress*

I can give you a six-word formula for success: Think things through—then follow through.
                                        —EDDIE RICKENBACKER

There are two kinds of stress: distress and good stress.

Distress stinks. Good stress is wonderful.

Good stress is positive stress. It allows you to turn your motor up and puts the rose-colored glasses on your face. It gives you a smile; it makes you feel good.

Distress, on the other hand, hurts you. You feel it when obstacles seem insurmountable or when you've done something wrong.

I don't have any distress. I won't permit it, just like I won't permit recession to impede my sales goals. It just doesn't get to me.

There are certain times when I can't resist the power of distress, like when my father died. I was distressed when he died, but I turned it into good stress.

How?

I turned it into happiness. I wasn't happy that he died, but I made it a positive thing. My father's still with me. I wear his ring to this day. I put it on the day he died, many years ago, and I've never taken it off. I still hear his voice and feel his guidance.

That is how I have good stress from my dad. He's still with me, and he'll never go away.

I watched a television show recently that told the story of a man who had to pull the plug on his brother because he had been in a serious car accident and would never regain consciousness. The show caused me to relive my whole life with my father. That hurt. My father was killed when he was struck by a car.

But stress can be wonderfully effective if handled wisely. For instance, I always have butterflies in my stomach before speaking to large groups. I bet few professional performers can go on stage without feeling the same stress. The secret is this: With a loser, stress takes over and controls the situation, but a winner manages stress and uses it to his or her advantage. As a result, the winner does a perfect job.

147

That's the secret to using stress. Once the announcer says, "Ladies and gentlemen, presenting Sid Friedman," I force the butterflies to shape up and fly together.

Distress cripples; good stress powers.

Stress management applies when you try to make a sale, too. As soon as you walk in, you must manage those butterflies. Stress won't go away completely, but you can keep it to a minimum through a complete program of learning, being prepared, and knowing what you're going to say before you say it.

Managing stress is an important skill that is developed over time.

••

Trade Secret #97

Rating Relationships on "The Tension Meter"

At the beginning of a presentation to a prospect, relationship tension is high because the prospect is often suspicious and uncertain of who the salesperson is and of what is being sold. In addition, the salesperson is often not sure of what the prospect thinks or best way to approach him or her.

Midway through the presentation, relationship tension goes down and task tension goes up because the prospect feels reassured and is less uncertain. By then the salesperson has sized up the prospect and has adapted his or her approach to suit the client.

Your job as a salesperson is to push the relationship tension down first; then you can deal with the task.

••

57 *Be Prepared for Getting Knocked Off Course*

If the bull had no horns, everyone would be a matador.
—ANONYMOUS

Your chances of being knocked off course are about 100 percent guaranteed. It might be some disaster, catastrophe, or tragedy; or it could be something minor, inconsequential, or petty. But it's bound to happen—and more than once. Maybe many times.

If you try to guess what might go wrong, you'll guess incorrectly. Whatever actually does happen will be different than what you expected, and probably worse, too. But no matter what happens, you must fix it or go around it. Don't ever accept the worst; just accept that it's going to happen.

At one point in my life, I had three big problems at the same time. I found out that I had life-threatening cancer. At the same time, my father—my best friend—died in a terrible accident. And I learned that my 13-year-old daughter was on drugs.

How's that for obstacles to throw me off course?

Many people would have fallen apart. But I made a conscious decision to fight back and not allow one of those nightmares to consume me. I accepted them for what they were, but they didn't beat me.

I helped my daughter through some very tough love. She's no longer on drugs.

I accepted that my father died and dealt with that as best I could.

And, of course, I beat the cancer.

Any one of those three could have torn me up and sent me down. Maybe it did for a while. I don't know. But I don't think so.

My solution was to fight back. Work harder. Just accept that it happened but deny it the power to defeat. That doesn't mean I ignored finding a solution to the problem. It means I ignored the distress of the problem.

At first, the bridge I used to get over the problems was to imagine that dad didn't die, that my daughter wasn't on drugs, and that

149

I wasn't sick with cancer. I had faith and kept dreaming. Eventually all those potentially crippling troubles went away.

Your perception is your reality.

....

Trade Secret #98

Anticipate Objections

The best defense to strong objections from a prospect is *not* a good offense. Some sales experts claim that a strong comeback is the most effective way to neutralize an objection.

I disagree.

Instead, I've found that the best way to reduce the negative impact of a strong objection is to *anticipate it and be prepared for it.*

Most objections have merit. Demonstrate your understanding of the problem before you offer your solution.

....

Trade Secret #99

Five Tips for Working With Prospects

When working with a prospect, remember to:

1. Be confident by preparing well

2. Set the prospect up quickly

3. Make it easy

4. Be quiet and wait patiently for responses

5. Move in and show that you expect action

....

58 Guests and Hosts

In adversity remember to keep an even mind.

—Horace

Someone once observed that there are two kinds of people in the world: guests and hosts.

The guests tend to walk in, plop themselves down, and expect to be taken care of by others. They are primarily concerned about their own interests, needs, and desires. They make lousy communicators.

Hosts, on the other hand, are sensitive to the feelings and needs of others. They concentrate on others rather than always thinking about themselves. Their actions are designed to make others feel at home, and they have potential for being great communicators.

Work hard to find ways to be a host.

You'll make many more sales by being a host, and, if you are like me, you'll also enjoy your work (and your play) more.

Trade Secret #100

Adapting Your Approach to the Personality of Your Prospect

To raise your success level, you've got to tune into the personality type of your prospect and adapt your own personality to suit. Here are some suggestions:

- Change your personality to develop rapport with different types of people.
- If you're uncomfortable with another personality type, practice changing.
- Bring a person to your presentation who's more like the prospect.
- Use your first visit for fact-finding: learn what type of person the prospect is. Then you'll know how to adapt your style when you come back—or an appropriate person to bring along.

- Begin your presentation by matching the prospect's style, and then gradually shift your approach to get the prospect to be more comfortable with the approach that feels most comfortable to you. (For example, if you speak rapidly and the other person speaks slowly, begin speaking slowly. Then gradually increase your pace and you'll find that the other person will match you.)
- Rearrange your presentation folder or use different illustrations and demonstrations according to the prospect's style of listening and comprehension.
- Practice a variety of approaches to individuals with each personality type. Then you'll be ready to use the most appropriate approach when the time comes.
- Research or take classes to learn more about the wants and needs of individuals with different personality types.

••

Trade Secret #101

Financial Speed

The sooner you start saving, the slower you can go, and the more you can enjoy the journey.

Suppose you wanted to save $1 million by investing $20,000 annually.

The table below shows how long it would take at various interest rates compounded annually.

Time Needed To Save $1 Million (with $20,000 annual investment)	
Annual Return	Years
0%	50
5%	25
6%	23
7%	22
8%	20
10%	18
12%	17
15%	15

The table below shows various yields on tax-deferred/tax-free insurance policies and the rates required to earn the same amount when the investment isn't tax-deferred/tax-free (based on 33 percent tax bracket).

Tax-Deferred Tax-Free	Pre-Tax Equivalent
6%	9%
8%	12%
10%	15%

How much risk do you want to take to earn the equivalent interest rates?

59 *Grind It Out*

A man must make his opportunity, as oft as find it.
—FRANCIS BACON

You probably know how lavish and opulent the casinos are.

I don't care where you go to gamble: Atlantic City, Las Vegas, the Bahamas, Europe. The casinos are gorgeous. The people are beautiful. The food is fabulous.

Do you know why?

It's because the casinos will do anything to get you there. They know, mathematically, that once you are there and gambling, they're automatic winners.

Casinos make money—without fail.

The more million dollar jackpots they pay out, the more money they make. The big jackpots draw more gamblers, and the more gamblers, the more profits.

The casino owners know that, over the long haul, players have to lose. Without exception. In craps, for example, the house is happy with a 0.5 percent edge. A half a penny out of every dollar wagered pays for an awful lot of overhead. (Did I say the house was "happy?" Hell, "thrilled to death" is more like it.)

Even if you get into a game and win thousands of dollars, the casino is still happy with your action because over the course of hours, days, and weeks, the correct mathematical odds will come into play, and then they'll earn their 0.5 percent on tens of millions of dollars.

Win, lose, or draw, they always win. Gamblers call it the grind.

"They're grindin' me down, slow but sure," is the lament you'll hear at an ice cold craps table. You never hear it at a hot table, yet it is just as true. It's just harder to see.

What does all of this have to do with selling life insurance?

Plenty.

With selling insurance, *you* have to do the grinding.

You have to believe (because it is true!) that you need to make 100 cold calls to get ten appointments. Out of the ten appointments, five will stand you up. Out of the other five, three will have their reasons why they can't buy.

And one or two *will* buy.

Of those who do buy, you'll average about $500 in commission. That's 500 bucks for 100 telephone calls, which equals $5 per call. Imagine how that thought changes your perspective as you begin a week's calls.

"Hello," you say as you make your first call of the week.

The prospect says "no way," and hangs up on you.

You shout, "Thank you!" into the dead telephone because you just earned $5.

On your next call, someone says, "Get lost!"

"Thanks for the $5!" you say.

The next call says, "I'm already over-insured."

"Thanks!" you reply.

"My brother-in-law is a State Farm agent," is the next rejection.

"Great! Thank you! Thank you! Thank you!" you say, in total sincerity. After all, you just earned another $5.

Am I kidding?

Absolutely not. The math of selling hasn't changed at all. But your attitude sure has.

And it keeps on getting better and better.

••

Trade Secret #102

Don't Pass the Repast

Taking a prospect out to lunch or dinner (or being invited out by the prospect) gives you an excellent opportunity to build on the relationship.

Always take advantage of these golden opportunities.

Sharing a meal or any other social activity gives you the chance to reduce the relationship tension and increase the task tension.

••

Trade Secret #103

How Will the Estate Taxes Be Paid?

The table on the next page shows options for paying estate taxes of $1 million projected liability.

Option	Cost	Comments
Sell or liquidate assets	$1 million plus	Loss of assets, growth and income*
Savings and cash reserve	$1 million plus	Loss of cash interest, and flexibility
Borrow	$1 million plus	Loss of principal plus interest
Insurance (discounted dollars)	$20,000/year for 10 years	Loss of interest only

*If real estate must be sold to pay estate taxes, it might be necessary to sell $3 million or $4 million worth of property in order to net $1 million in cash after paying off the mortgage, the sales commission, and any other selling expenses. The commission and other selling expenses alone might exceed the cost of life insurance.

••

60 *Grandma's Lesson*

Keep the faculty of effort alive in you by a little gratuitous exercise every day.

—WILLIAM JAMES

For another example about hanging in there, I often think of my grandma's old-fashioned meat grinder.

She bolted the grinder to her table, and she bought the best quality meat. She put the meat in the top and held it down with a wooden spoon so it wouldn't pop out. If she held the meat down and turned the handle hard and long enough, only one thing could happen: the meat would *have* to come out the other end.

It had to come out as ground steak.

Well, prospecting is the same process.

Just as grandma secured the meat grinder and bought quality meat, you must secure a good list of prospects—a good group of names—and put it on your desk.

Then you must put the meat in the top of the grinder. That means, get to the phone and start dialing. Like grandma, you must hold the meat down—keep making the phone calls—so that it has nowhere to go but out the other end. Calling turns quality prospects into quality sales.

Most importantly, you have to remember to turn the handle like hell. Keep turning and turning and the more you turn, the more the process will work. Having good prospects is only part of it. You have to turn the handle as well. Give the system a motor, the discipline, by turning the handle and doing it all the time. Keep putting the meat in and turning the handle, and the meat will come out. Keep doing that and it'll happen.

Grandma knew not to stop.

She knew how to make good chopped steak by putting quality meat in. Then she added onions, some bread, spices, and other things because the chopped meat alone didn't taste as good. You can add career education, closing techniques, persistence, and whatever spices you want to your personal recipe.

You start putting ingredients in the pot by getting the right-sized group of prospects, the right-sized business, and the right place in

157

town. You will develop a reputation and soon be making chopped steak that's fabulous because it's high quality. Then you sit back and enjoy it.

Again, the key is to keep finding new prospects and turning the handle. You will be successful sooner than you think.

That's what you have to do.

••

Trade Secret #104

Learn To Wait after Asking a Closing Question

After you ask a closing question, the first and most important rule is to shut up! The first person to talk at this point loses. Let the prospect give you the answers.

Then, turn any questions back on your prospect with other questions. For example:

They say: Does it come in red?

You say: Do you want it in red?

When they say yes, that's a close.

Lastly, back off and wait. Then the prospect doesn't feel pressured. You need to give him or her space to answer. Give the prospect 10 seconds of silence to plant the hook. Let the answer come from the prospect.

Learn to wait!

••

This Book's Ultimate Message

I'd be happy if the final impressions this book leaves on you are that, no matter what happens, no matter what the conditions are, no matter how many mountains you have to climb, you come to believe in the power of never letting up and the truth behind the saying, "If it is to be, it is up to me."

Believing these ten little words could change your life and make you a millionaire quicker than you probably imagine. I'm not pretending to be a prophet, but those ten words ring absolutely true.

If it is to be, it is up to me.

One Final Word

Now that you've read this book, what do you do?

What comes next?

How do you get going and put some of these proven ideas to work for you, immediately?

Press the start button!

My friend Shelly Pressler told me about how he gets started every morning. On the floor of his office he has a bright red, four-foot replica of a start button.

Every morning, just before his work day begins, he and one of his associates sprint across the office and leap, feet first, onto the start button. That officially begins their work day. I heartily recommend this method to all who need help in getting started.

And once you start, *please,* never let up.

Index

Insurance Training Courses

		Order Number	Price	Quantity	Total Amount
1.	*Survey of Advanced Sales	5408-04	$31.95		
2.	*Business Insurance	5412-06	$49.95		
3.	*Estate Planning	5414-09	$49.95		
4.	*Pensions & Profit Sharing	5415-14	$49.95		
5.	*Investment Planning	5205-03	$49.95		
6.	*Income Tax Planning	5206-15	$49.95		
7.	*Disability Income Insurance	5426-02	$32.95		
8.	*Medicare Supplement Insurance	5440-21	$18.95		
9.	*Key Executive Benefits	5445-01	$18.95		
10.	*403(b) Plans	5464-01	$18.95		
11.	*Variable Universal Life	5435-01	$18.95		
12.	*401(k) Plans	5437-01	$18.95		
13.	*Buy-Sell Agreements	5438-01	$18.95		
14.	*Section 125 Cafeteria Plans	5439-01	$18.95		
15.	*Charitable Giving Through Life Insurance	5440-01	$18.95		
16.	*Simplified Employee Pension Plans (SEPs)	5463-01	$18.95		
17.	*Qualified Retirement Plans (QRPs)	5460-01	$18.95		
18.	*Individual Retirement Accounts (IRAs)	5462-01	$18.95		
19.	*Rollovers	5461-01	$18.95		

*To receive state insurance continuing education credit, a $25.00 grading service fee is required. To enroll:
Call toll-free 1-800-621-9621, ext. 652. In Illinois, call 1-312-836-4400, ext. 652.

Insurance Selling

20.	**High Touch Selling** by John Savage	2401-24	$19.95	
21.	**Common-Sense Selling** by Joe Casale	2401-25	$16.95	
22.	**Creative Selling for the 1990s**, Revised, by Ben Feldman	2401-04	$18.95	
23.	**Clients First!** by Joseph D. Citarella	2401-27	$19.95	
24.	**Special Limited Edition Feldman**	2401-03	$59.95	
25.	**Ben Feldman at Work** (2 audio tapes)	2418-01	$19.95	
26.	**The Best of Ben** (5 booklets)	2418-04	$10.95	
27.	**The Feldman Method**, Revised, by Andrew H. Thompson with Lee Rosler	2401-12	$18.95	
28.	**The Insurance Dictionary**, 3rd Edition by John R. Ingrisano	5602-16	$19.95	
29.	**World Class Selling** by Art Mortell	2401-28	$19.95	
30.	**How to Make Money Tomorrow Morning** by Sidney A. Friedman	2401-29	$19.95	

Reference for Financial Professionals

31.	**Section 403(b) Manual**, 8th Edition, by Arvid L. Mortensen	5605-02	$37.95	
32.	**The Deferred Compensation Handbook** by Stephan Leimberg and Linda Feldman	2402-31	$32.95	
33.	**The IRA Manual,** 2nd Edition by Norman H. Tarver and Arvid L. Mortensen	5605-01	$35.95	
34.	**Power Marketing** by Richard Wollack and Alan Parisse	1916-08	$29.95	
35.	**The Mutual Fund Encyclopedia** by Gerald W. Perritt	5608-23	$27.95	
36.	**Tax Companion 1991**	5606-01	$14.95	
37.	**Pocket Tables 1991** (package of 50)	5606-32	$27.50	

Shipping and Handling Charges	
Total Purchase	Charge
$ 0.00-$24.99	$4.00
$ 25.00-$49.99	$5.00
$ 50.00-$99.99	$6.00
$100.00-$249.99	$8.00

Also available at your local bookstore.

Orders shipped to the following states must include applicable sales tax: CA, CO, FL, IL, MI, MN, NY, PA, TX and WI.

Subtotal _____

Applicable Sales Tax _____

Shipping and Handling Charges _____

Total _____

$20.00 Minimum Order

Prices subject to change without notice

ORDER TODAY! CALL TOLL-FREE
1-800-621-9621 ext. 650. In Illinois 1-312-836-4400 ext. 650.
Or FAX your order 1-312-836-1021.

Place your order today! Call toll-free 1-800-621-9621, ext. 650. In Illinois, call 1-312-836-4400, ext. 650. Mention code 830321. Or FAX your order: 1-312-836-1021.

Please send me the books indicated on the reverse side of this order form:

☐ Payment enclosed
 Make check payable to:
Dearborn Financial Publishing, Inc.
Charge to:

☐ VISA ☐ MasterCard

Card No. _____

Exp. Date _____

Signature _____
(All charge orders must be signed)

Name _____

Company _____

Street Address _____

City _____

State _____ Zip _____

Business Phone ( )_____

Return Address:

_____
_____
_____

PLACE
STAMP
HERE

 Dearborn
Financial Publishing, Inc.
Order Department
520 North Dearborn Street
Chicago, Illinois 60610-4354

IMPORTANT—PLEASE FOLD OVER—PLEASE TAPE BEFORE MAILING

30-Day Guarantee
All Dearborn Financial Publishing, Inc.
publications come with a 30-day money-back guarantee.
If for any reason you aren't completely satisfied,
just return your order for a full refund or credit, no questions asked.

NOTE: This page, when folded over and taped, becomes an envelope, which has been approved by the United States Postal Service. It is provided for your convenience.

Dearborn Financial Publishing, Inc.
520 N. Dearborn St. Chicago, IL 60610   Where Experts Begin